# DE VALERA'S DARKEST HOUR:
In Search of National Independence,
1919–1932

# *De Valera's Darkest Hour:*
## *In Search of National Independence 1919–1932*

### T. RYLE DWYER

THE MERCIER PRESS
DUBLIN and CORK

The Mercier Press Limited
4 Bridge Street, Cork
24 Lower Abbey Street, Dublin 1

© T. Ryle Dwyer, 1982

ISBN 0 85342 676 7

To Barney O'Connor

*Cover photograph: BBC Hulton Picture Library.*

*Printed by Litho Press Co. Midleton, Co. Cork.*

# Contents

| | | |
|---|---|---|
| Preface | | 7 |
| 1 | More Wilsonian than Wilson<br>*Internationalising the Irish Question* | 9 |
| 2 | Not Enough Room for the Judge<br>*The Irish Split in America* | 30 |
| 3 | Dominion Status or the Status of a Dominion<br>*Negotiating with the British* | 53 |
| 4 | No Right to Do Wrong<br>*Events Leading to the Civil War* | 81 |
| 5 | All the Public Responsibility<br>*The Civil War* | 118 |
| 6 | Regaining the Citadel<br>*From Prison to the Presidency* | 149 |
| Notes | | 174 |
| Bibliography | | 183 |
| Index | | 186 |

# Acknowledgements

I would like to thank the staffs of the various institutions for their help, especially those at the Kerry County Library, National Library of Ireland, State Paper Office, Trinity College and University College, Dublin; National Archives, Washington, D.C.; New York City Public Library; Marquette University, University of Wisconsin (Parkside); University of Illinois (Chicago); the National Archives of Canada, Ottawa. I would also like to thank various people for their help and hospitality, my brother Seán and his wife Geraldine, Therese Hassett, Fr Anthony Gaughan, Nanette Barrett, Liam Collins, Michael Costello, Ger Power, John Lawlor, Joe O'Shea, Paddy Barry, Declan Keane, Tom Wallace, and Bob MacSweeney. Finally I would like to thank my mother, Margaret R. Dwyer, for reading the manuscript in all its stages.

T.R.D.
*Tralee*

# Preface

During the Civil War and afterwards Eamon de Valera was accused of the most outrageous crimes. He was widely depicted as the instigator and, indeed, the perpetrator of that civil conflict, with the result that he was probably the most despised man in all of Ireland. Had he been caught during the fighting, the prognosis for the long life he eventually lived, would not have been good. The best he could have hoped for would have been a summary court martial and swift execution. When he was eventually apprehended while speaking at a public meeting after the conclusion of hostilities, the government decided that he should be brought to trial as quickly as possible. But the only hard evidence of any alleged crime that Free State authorities could come up with was the utterly ludicrous charge of having supposedly incited Cumann na mBan during the Civil War. In the light of all he had been accused of, it was not surprising that he was never brought to trial.

This, then, is the story of de Valera's struggle for national independence during the most controversial period of his career, from his election as Priomh Aire of Dáil Éireann, his unauthorised assumption of the title of President, his controversial tour of the United States, his obscure part in the negotiations leading to the Anglo-Irish Treaty, his reasons for rejecting the Treaty, his misunderstood role in the period leading up to and during the Civil War, and finally his spectacular recovery in lifting himself from the despised depths of 1923 to become President of the Executive Council of the Irish Free State in less than nine years.

CHAPTER ONE

# More Wilsonian than Wilson

## *Internationalising the Irish Question*

On 1 April 1919 Eamon de Valera was elected *Priomh Aire* of Dáil Éireann, the Irish revolutionary assembly which had been established some months earlier by the members of Sinn Féin who had refused to sit at Westminster. Having named the members of his government he gave an interview to a correspondent of the London *Daily Herald*.

Stressing that Sinn Féin was not an isolationist party, de Valera explained that the organisation's name should be translated, 'We Ourselves', rather than the more frequently used 'Ourselves Alone', which he felt smacked of isolationism. Instead of 'desiring isolation', he emphasised that the Sinn Féin struggle was to get Ireland 'recognised as an independent unit in a world-league of nations.'[1]

De Valera's international outlook was understandable seeing that he obviously owed his own freedom to the force of international opinion. Less than three years earlier he had been sentenced to life-in-prison for his part in the Easter Rebellion, but the British released him and his colleagues after little more than a year in an obvious effort to curry favour with American opinion. He and his colleagues then lost no time in making it clear to the world that they intended to continue their struggle for Irish freedom. They wrote an open letter to the American President, Woodrow Wilson, with an appeal to 'the Government of the United States of America, and the governments of the free peoples of the world to take immediate measures to inform themselves accurately and on the spot about the extent of liberty or attempted repression which we may encounter.'[2]

As the Easter Rebellion had been a dismal failure militarily, de Valera believed Ireland's best hope of securing her independence would be at the Peace Conference following the conclusion of the First World War, but he realised it would first be necessary to claim independence in order to get a hearing at that conference. It was as republicans, he felt, the Irish would have the best chance of success because, with the exception of Britain, the major Allied nations like the United States, France, and Russia (then under the Provisional Government of Alexander Kerensky) were all republics.

Working largely behind the scenes de Valera managed to persuade the fragmented Irish separatist movement to coalesce under a republican banner within the Sinn Féin Party, with himself as leader in October 1917. He even induced the monarchist Arthur Griffith, the party's founder, to step aside and accept the republican formula on the understanding that once the republic had been secured, the Irish people would 'by referendum freely choose their own form of government.'[3]

De Valera then began touring the country on behalf of the party. His message was clear. If necessary, he was prepared to support 'active resistence' against British rule, but only if a passive policy in the form of an appeal to the Peace Conference first proved unsuccessful. 'We cannot give a guarantee that we are going to be successful,' he admitted, but he nevertheless thought the country's best hope lay in securing the support of the United States at the Peace Conference.[4]

'President Wilson has distinguished very carefully between solid substance and loud, high-sounding phrases,' de Valera said, 'and we shall see if his own phrases are going to be hollow and high-sounding with no solid substance behind them.'[5] Yet he was not just relying on Wilson; he also planned to call on the Irish in the United States to use their influence on Ireland's behalf. 'Those extremists, those who want Ireland a nation in reality, and in truth are,' he explained, 'the great bulk of the Irish in the States, and their weighty influence it is that will yet help to squeeze John Bull. The Irish have gone with a vengeance which they will not forget to repay; only let us show them that we here at home have not abandoned their ideals or given up the hopes which inspired them in the past, and brightened their exile.'6

There could be no doubt such talk was questioning Wilson's sincerity. 'If President Wilson is honest, he will easily pardon us for not trusting him with an implicit faith,' de Valera candidly asserted. 'If he is a hypocrite — if he is a meet partner for those who began this world war with altrustic professions of liberty and freedom, then the sooner Americans and the sooner mankind knows it the better.'7

Emphasising he was not making a premature judgment, the Sinn Féin leader declared that Wilson would 'by his actions, pronounce a judgment upon himself.' Ireland was going to be the test which 'would prove to the world the sincerity or hypocrisy of the Allies, and President Wilson, when they declared that they were fighting for the self-determination of nations.'8 De Valera had already stated that if earnest proof were furnished that Ireland was being included amongst those small nations for whose rights the Allies were supposedly fighting, a half-million Irishmen would be ready to co-operate with the Allies. 'Then they will find,' he said, 'that these half-a-million men will be ready to defend their own land and ready, to give a helping hand to the oppressed.'9 As far as he was concerned the Allies could easily 'prove their sincerity by giving to the Irish people the right of self-determination.'10

'We here in Ireland are fighting in our own way, the only way open to us — for the principle of self-determination,' de Valera contended. If that was really what the United States was fighting for, as Wilson declared, then Ireland and America were 'genuine "associates" in this war', with the result that Ireland should therefore receive from the United States and her 'President that sympathy and that active support which the community of our aims entitles us to expect.'11 By thus associating the Irish question with the Great War, the most emotive international issue of the day, the Sinn Féin leader was trying to depict the Irish cause in the most favourable international light.

Nevertheless Sinn Féin initially made little headway under de Valera's leadership. The party lost the first three by-elections it contested in early 1918. Things were looking bad until the British began making moves towards the introduction of conscription in Ireland. A conscription bill was rushed through the British parliament in less than a week over the vociferous objections of members of the Irish Parliamentary Party who were left in impotent frustration. They withdrew from Westminster in protest and returned to Ireland, where their actions were seen as tantamount to endorsing the abstentionist policy being advocated by Sinn Féin.

A conference of the various Irish nationalist groups was convened on 18 April 1918 at the Mansion House, Dublin, where the Sinn Féin leader had a profound influence on the meeting, which adopted a declaration bearing the indelible imprint of separatist thinking. Basing the case against conscription on 'Ireland's separate and distinct nationhood' together with the principle that governments 'derive their just powers from the consent of the governed', the declaration denied 'the right of the British Government, or any external authority, to impose compulsory service in Ireland against the clearly expressed will of the Irish people.' At de Valera's suggestion the conference enlisted the support of the Roman Catholic hierarchy, which virtually sanctified the campaign against conscription by directing that the clergy celebrate a special Mass the following Sunday 'in every church in Ireland to avert the scourge of conscription with which Ireland is now threatened.'[12]

The Sinn Féin leader also exploited the conscription issue to secure international publicity by giving his first newspaper interview ever to a correspondent of the *Christian Science Monitor*. During the interview he explained that the Irish people were anxious to remain aloof from the world conflict. As they had no independent means of determining 'the relative guilt of the nations in bringing about this war,' he said the people were not prepared to accept that the Germans or their associates were in the wrong, with the result that Ireland had no moral obligation to enter the fray. Although the principles put forward by the American President were undoubtedly ones that 'in the abstract should commend themselves to all right-thinking men,' de Valera stressed that the British leadership did not fit that category, because if Britain were sincere in supporting those Wilsonian principles, 'she could apply them without trouble and without delay' in Ireland's case.[13]

When the interviewer asked about the possibility of the United States ensuring that Ireland would be fairly treated after the war if the Irish people wholeheartedly threw their lot in with the Allies, de Valera dismissed the idea, as he would later dismiss it during the Second World War and even later again when the possibility of a third World War was being seriously considered. 'Ireland cannot afford to gamble,' he replied. 'Great powers strong enough to enforce their contracts can safely enter a combination, knowing their strength is a guarantee that the contract will not be violated and that what they stipulated for will not be denied them when success is achieved.' A small nation, on the other hand, would 'have no such guarantee' as its allies could 'deny it that for which it fought, and substitute, in the end, principles other than, and quite different from, those enunciated at the outset.' In other words, as he later explained, 'We are a nation of four and a half millions; we could be cheated in the end; but America is too big a nation, and America has to look nowhere else but to itself for guarantees that it won't be cheated.'[14]

De Valera was not content with simply relying on an American newspaper interview. He also prepared a formal appeal to the United States on behalf of the Mansion House Conference. Having drafted the text, he circulated it among the other conference members but before further action could be taken, he and several other prominent members of Sinn Féin were arrested for reputed involvement in a supposed German Plot. As the British never produced any convincing evidence that such a plot existed, there was great scepticism about the charges. To most Irish people it seemed that Britain was just taking the Sinn Féiners out of circulation because they were proving a political embarrassment. De Valera was certainly not involved in any such plot, but he was deported and spent most of the next nine months in Lincoln Gaol.

Sinn Féin made the most of the propaganda potential afforded by the arrests. An edited version of de Valera's appeal to the United States was published in pamphlet form.[15] It ended in mid-sentence, as if he had been arrested with pen in hand while actually drafting the document. Since only members of Sinn Féin were arrested, people inevitably concluded that British authorities thought that Sinn Féin was primarily responsible for organising the widespread opposition to conscription, with the result that the party profited most from the popular backlash generated by the issue, which ultimately dealt the fatal political blow to the moribund Irish Parliamentary Party.

When the Great War ended in November 1918 de Valera still had high hopes that Ireland would find an influential ally in President Wilson, who had continued to speak in idealistic terms during the final year of the war. In February 1918 the American President had re-asserted that national aspirations would have to be respected if there was to be a lasting peace. '"Self-determination" is not a mere phrase,' he said. 'It is an imperative principle of action, which statesmen will henceforth ignore at their peril.'[16]

'If America holds to the principles enunciated by her President during the war she will have a noble place in the history of nations,' de Valera wrote to his mother from Lincoln Gaol on 28 November 1918. He was convinced those Wilsonian principles could be 'the basis of true statecraft — a firm basis that will bear the stress of time — but will the President be able to get them accepted by others whose entry into the war was on motives less unselfish?'

'What an achievement should he succeed in getting established a common law for nations — resting on the will of the nations — making national duals as rare as duals between individual persons are at present,' de Valera continued; 'if that be truly his aim, may God steady his hand.'[17]

Any real doubts that may have existed about the Irish desire for self-government were largely dispelled with the results of a general election held on 14 December 1918 when Sinn Féin candidates — having clearly indicated in their election manifesto that they would not sit at Westminster but would establish instead their own republican assembly in Ireland — won 73 seats against 26 for the

Unionists, and only six for the once powerful Parliamentary Party. Then six weeks later those Sinn Féin representatives who were not in jail, established Dáil Éireann, which immediately adopted a Declaration of Independence, re-affirmed the establishment of the Irish Republic first proclaimed during the Easter Rebellion, and voted to appoint de Valera, Griffith, and George Noble Count Plunkett as representatives to the Peace Conference in Paris.

Preparations were already well under way to help de Valera escape from Lincoln Gaol. Two of the party's young activists, Michael Collins and Harry Boland, went over to Lincoln to supervise the escape attempt, which was successfully executed on the night of 3 February 1919. De Valera then secretly returned to Ireland but revealed that his stay would only be temporary as he intended to go to the United States in order to drum up American support for the Irish cause.

There were soon encouraging signs from the United States. Just before the existing Congress dissolved on 4 March 1919, the House of Representatives adopted a resolution advocating that the Peace Conference should 'favourably consider the claims of Ireland to the right of self-determination.' The resolution was really, however, only a symbolic gesture, as the Wilson administration had managed to get the vote delayed until after the Senate had dissolved, so it did not therefore vote on the measure. Nevertheless the gesture was an indication that notwithstanding what many people viewed as Sinn Féin's pro-German attitude during the war, sympathy for Ireland was still strong in the United States.

From his hiding place in Dublin de Valera endorsed the various efforts to enlist the help of 'President Wilson whose clear enunciation of the true principles of international rights had kindled throughout Ireland the firmest confidence in an early restoration of her inalienable liberties.' Although some people already suspected Wilson's willingness to discard those principles, especially in regard to Ireland, the Sinn Féin leader called for patience. 'Pronounce no opinion on President Wilson,' he cautioned. 'It is premature, for he and his friends will bear our country in mind at the crucial hour.'[18]

It was not long, however, before there were indications that all was not well in Paris. De Valera, who was able to come out of hiding when those being held for their supposed part in the German Plot were released, publicly warned the Dáil that there were signs the proposed League of Nations was taking on the aspects of an organisation designed to preserve the status quo. It seemed those in Paris were losing sight of Wilson's principles. In particular, de Valera warned that France seemed bent on imposing vindictive peace terms on Germany.

'We must try to save France from herself,' he said. The new treaty would be violated like the Franco-German Treaty of 1871 and another war of revenge would surely follow. 'Therefore, while we can sympathise with France, and understand her attitude, we must remember that, as far as that country is concerned, she is suffering from too many terrible wounds to be calm at present. It is for those who have suffered less to compose France and to try to save her from an act that would endanger her future.'

Ireland was ready to play her role in securing a lasting peace, he declared. 'We are ready to enter and take part in a League of Nations founded on equality and right among nations.' However, if the Covenant of the proposed League were to be lasting, he said it should 'be based on the principles which occupied ten of the fourteen points of President Wilson — the rights of every nation to self-determination. We take up these principles because they are right, and we take them up particularly because the acceptance of these principles will mean that the long fight for Irish liberty is at an end.'[19]

Following the publication of the draft terms of the Versailles Treaty in early May 1919, it became painfully obvious that Ireland was not going to get a hearing at Paris, so de Valera reverted to what his authorised biographers described as 'his original plan of going to America and appealing to the people above the head of Woodrow Wilson.'[20] A formal perfunctory request was made for a hearing at the Peace Conference and de Valera then stowed away on a ship bound for the United States.

While he was en route there was a very significant development when the United States Senate adopted a resolution introduced by Senator William Borah of Idaho requesting the American delegation in Paris to secure a hearing at the Peace Conference for de Valera and his two colleagues 'in order that they may present the cause of Ireland'. The resolution, which was passed by sixty votes to one, added 'that the Senate of the United States expresses its sympathy with the aspirations of the Irish people for a Government of their own choice.'[21] The senators knew the resolution was a futile move, but as a gesture of sympathy it was of enormous significance seeing that any treaty which Wilson would bring back from Paris was going to need the approval of two-thirds of the members of the United States Senate for ratification.

Upon his arrival the Irish leader anticipated sympathetic support, especially from Irish-Americans, who were probably more powerful than at any time in history. The Friends of Irish Freedom (FOIF), an organisation founded in March 1916 with the aim of fostering efforts 'to bring about the National Independence of Ireland',[22] had gained appreciable strength in recent months, with the result that de Valera expected assistance from an ally with strong political muscle.

As the Irish Republic had not been officially recognised, he saw his basic role in the United States as that of a propagandist, rather than a diplomat. Although he realised he was likely to clash with some Irish-Americans in that role, he decided to press on because, as he explained later, 'sentimental regard for the official position which I held would enable me to get a far wider audience for educational propaganda than any American. And then every reception given to me by public officials was a kind of formal recognition of the Republic.'[23] He was actually so conscious of the propaganda potential of his position that he allowed his title to be changed from *Priomh Aire* to President, without consulting his Dáil colleagues.[24] The new title had the obvious advantage of affording him a more impressive platform from which to appeal to Americans.

In addition to his main aim of securing official recognition, he had a number of other goals, one being raising money for the independence movement by selling Irish Republican bonds. He also hoped to smooth over some difference developing within Irish-American ranks.

During the year and a half he was in the United States, de Valera travelled extensively and attracted as much public attention as possible, thereby securing a great deal of publicity for the Irish cause which would probably not have otherwise been forthcoming. As Irish leader, he was fêted throughout the country and was invited to address state legislatures in Massachusetts, New Jersey, Maryland, Delaware, Virginia, and Montana, in addition to being greeted by fourteen different state governors and by the mayors of some of the largest cities.

From the time of his initial American public appearance, de Valera seized on the opportunity of injecting Ireland into international politics by deliberately linking the Irish question with the growing political controversy over whether the United States should join the League of Nations.[25] Even before the signing of the Versailles Treaty, which contained the League Covenant, he revealed his intention of using the League of Nations issue to get the American people to put pressure on President Wilson to recognise the Irish Republic. He told a New York press conference:

> We shall fight for a real democratic League of Nations, not the present unholy alliance which does not fulfil the purposes for which the democracies of the world went to war. I am going to ask the American people to give us a real League of Nations, one that will include Ireland.
>
> I well recognise President Wilson's difficulties in Paris. I am sure that if he is sincere, nothing will please him more than being pushed from behind by the people, for this pressure will show him that the people of America want the United States Government to recognise the Republic of Ireland.
>
> This is the reason I am eager to spread propaganda in official circles in America. My appeal is to the people. I

know if they can be aroused government action will follow. That is why I intend visiting your large cities and talking directly to the people.[26]

The Versailles Treaty was duly signed on 28 June 1919 as de Valera was about to set out on a hectic speaking tour. Next day in Boston he addressed a gathering of some 50,000 people in Fenway Park, and the day after that he spoke to the Massachusetts State Legislature. This was followed by a speech to some 30,000 people in Manchester, New Hampshire, before he returned to speak to an overflow crowd at Madison Square Gardens, New York, where the police — mostly Irish-Americans — allowed people to stand in the isles in blatant contravention of fire regulations. As a result the estimated crowd of 17,000 was the largest ever crammed into the arena. On 13 July the Irish leader addressed some 25,000 people at Soldier's Field, Chicago. Next day, having met the Chicago City Council, he set out for San Francisco, where the Ancient Order of Hibernians was holding its convention. Following a brief stay in the San Francisco Bay area, he made a short visit to Montana, where he addressed the State Legislature, before returning to New York.

In little more than three weeks he had travelled from the Atlantic to the Pacific seaboards and back again, and had made seventeen major public addresses, in addition to numerous short talks at private functions. In the process he received enormous publicity, especially in the major daily newspapers of New York, Boston, Chicago, and San Francisco — all of which gave him prominent front page coverage, often with banner headlines and inside pages that were devoted almost exclusively to activities surrounding his visit.

Although de Valera repeatedly denounced the Versailles Treaty, he did so as a supporter rather than a critic of Wilsonian ideals. In Boston, for instance, he complained that the peace treaty was 'a mere mockery' which would lead to twenty wars instead of the one it had nominally ended. Unless the United States were willing to take the 'responsibility for the world to which her traditions entitle her,' he predicted mankind would be in for 'a period of misery for which history has no parallel.'[27]

'The present opportunity is never likely to occur again,' he explained. 'The idea of a unity of nations recognising a common law and a common right ending wars among nations is today a possibility if America will do what the people of the world look forward to, and expect her to do.' He wanted the United States to use its influence to get the treaty revised so the League of Nations could be based on the principle of national equality which, he contended, was the only basis on which the organisation would be likely to succeed.

The difficiencies of the treaty were manifold. While in Dublin de Valera had warned of the futility of expecting a lasting peace if vindictive terms were imposed on Germany. But he played down his objection on that score while in the United States. If he were going to be successful there as a propagandist for the Irish cause, it was important that he should avoid the taint of being an apologist for the Germans, as many Americans already believed the Sinn Féin movement had been too closely linked with Germany during the war.

De Valera therefore adopted a positive approach in trying to dispel Sinn Féin's unfavourable image by comparing the Irish rebels with both the patriots of the American revolution and the American soldiers who had just fought in the Great War. If he were an American, he said in Chicago, he would have felt obliged to serve in the United States Army during the recent conflict, in view of the country's avowed motives in entering the fray. 'I hold,' he added, 'that those of us who were fighting England were in reality fighting for the very principles for which the Americans fought.'[28]

When asked by an alderman of the Chicago City Council next day why members of Sinn Féin had remained aloof during the war, the Irish leader replied that first of all they did not think they were strong enough to ensure that their aim of securing freedom for small nations would be respected in Ireland's case, and secondly they were afraid that Britain would actually use their participation in the war to undermine the Irish struggle for independence. 'If we had gone in,' he explained, 'England would have made it appear we were in as England's partners and therefore content with England's occupation.'[29]

De Valera was careful to present his case in terms that appeared both consistent with American war aims and at the same time offset what seemed to be the betrayal of those aims at Versailles. He took particular exception to Article X of the Covenant, which committed members of the League 'to respect and preserve as against external aggression the territorial integrity' of fellow members. The clause was objectionable because it could be used by imperial nations to preserve the international *status quo*. If Americans subscribed to the proposed Covenant, he contended they would be placing their seal of approval on Britain's title to all her imperial possessions.

Before the Versailles Treaty was actually signed, de Valera told a New York press conference that the obnoxious implications of Article X could be rectified if the imperial powers would 'surrender their colonies and possessions as mandatories of the League.'[30] Basically therefore the Irish leader was not really opposed to Article X *per se*. And he made that clear in San Francisco, where he candidly recognised 'that if you are going to have a league of nations, you must have some article in it. . . like Article X, but it must be based on just conditions at the start.'[31]

The main problem, therefore, was the conditions under which the League was being founded. The Irish people were going to be dragged into the organisation as part of the United Kingdom, with the result that henceforth Article X could be used to deny Ireland the independence to which she was aspiring. The Covenant seemed to be the basis for a scheme to perpetuate the standing of the victorious empires, just like the Holy Alliance formed at the peace conference following the Napoleonic wars.

'A new "Holy Alliance" cannot save democracy,' de Valera declared in Boston. 'A just League of Nations, founded on the only basis on which it can be just — the equality of right among nations, small no less than great — can.' He added that 'America can see to it that such a league is set up and set up now. She is strong enough to do so, and it is her right, in consequence of the explicit terms on which she entered the war. . . . A covenant for a League of Nations can be formed at Washington as well as at Paris. Now is the time to frame it. It is not enough for you to destroy, you must build.'[32]

The Irish leader was not only speaking in terms that seemed distinctly Wilsonian, but he actually admitted privately that his strategy was to let President Wilson 'know that if he goes for his 14 points as they were and a true League of Nations, Irishmen and men and women of Irish blood will be behind him.'[33] Nevertheless there was a stark demonstration of just how bitterly disillusioned Irish-Americans were becoming with Wilson the following week, when the mere mention of the American President's name at the Madison Square Gardens meeting provoked a cacophony of disapproval as the crowd jeered, booed and hissed for over three minutes. The reaction was so strong that it made front page news as far away as Chicago, where the *Daily Tribune* afforded the incident a banner headline.[34]

While in Chicago a few days later de Valera obviously realised he had to soft-peddle his Wilsonian approach during the Soldier's Field meeting, which had already adopted a resolution declaring that it was 'unalterably opposed' to the Covenant. As this stand had been based on 'purely American grounds', he explained that he, 'as a stranger and as a guest here, could not presume to interfere.' He simply added that he personally objected to the League of Nations 'because it is going to do injustice to my country.' With the crowd strongly isolationist, he did not attempt to suggest the United States should actually enter the League with reservations.[35]

Throughout the country, however, the general tone of his speeches was quite different. To the horror of isolationists within Irish-American ranks, his addresses bore the indelible imprint of Wilsonian internationalism. In San Francisco the following week he told a gathering at City Hall that he was looking to the American people 'to make the world safe for democracy'.

'You can do it even now,' de Valera declared. 'If

America is determined to champion the cause of democracy in the world, that cause will triumph. If America leads the way towards true democracy, the democracy of England even, and of France and of Spain and every country in the world will follow your lead.' He proceeded to emphasise, with repetitious monotony, his own Wilsonian outlook. 'You are the only people that can lead,' he said, 'and if you lead, democracy will triumph and the world will indeed be safe for democracy.'[36]

Although the Irish leader's reception in the various cities was on the whole warm and sympathetic, there were some genuine misgivings in American circles about his mission. When analysed, for example, his basic objection to the Covenant seemed to be simply that Ireland was not being included as an independent member of the League from the start. While it would, of course, have been impolitic of him to have simply told Americans that they should oppose the League for basically Irish reasons, his fundamental argument was that the United States should not ratify the treaty because it would undermine the Irish struggle for independence.

When de Valera stated at his initial American press conference that he wanted 'a real League of Nations, one that will include Ireland', he seemed to be implying that his real objection to the Covenant was that Ireland was not being assured of a place as a separate nation in the League. Some months later in Philadelphia, he admitted that this was indeed his basic objection to the Covenant.[37]

Prominent Irish-Americans like John Devoy of the *Gaelic American* and Judge Daniel Cohalan, the effective leader of FOIF, based their objections to the Versailles Treaty on American grounds. Their opposition to the Covenant was much more intense than that of de Valera. As an ardent isolationist and a staunch anglophobe, Cohalan detested the idea of the United States surrendering any of her sovereignty, or freedom of action, to an international organisation like the League of Nations, especially when Britain would, in effect, have six votes to one of the United States as Britain's five dominions were each being accorded a vote. Contending that joining the League would be contrary to the traditional American policy of avoiding 'permanent, entangling alliances with any of the countries of the Old World,' he used the resources of FOIF to organise a very efficient Irish-American lobby against the League.[38]

Wilson sought to overcome such opposition by appealing directly to the American people. He set out on a nation-wide tour during which he intimated that Irish fears about Article X were groundless because the article did not apply to struggles of liberation. He even implied that the Covenant would actually enhance Irish prospects of securing international assistance, as the United States would be able to press Ireland's case for self-determination at the Council of the League of Nations under the provisions of Article XI, which, he said, stipulated that 'every matter which is likely to affect the peace of the world is everybody's business.'

'In other words,' Wilson added, 'at present we have to mind our own business. Under the Covenant of the League of Nations we can mind other people's business, and anything that affects the peace of the world, whether we are parties to it or not, can, by our delegates, be brought to the attention of mankind.'[39]

De Valera quickly countered those arguments by issuing statements contending that fears concerning Article X were not baseless. He had already acknowledged that the controversial article specifically referred to external aggression rather than revolutions, but he argued that the qualification really made little practical difference, because it would be used to prohibit outside aid and would thus strangle the struggle for Irish freedom. 'There is scarcely a single instance of where a revolution from within, alone and without external aid, was ever successful,' he explained. 'Article X of the League of Nations would cut off Ireland from such sympathy.' In emphasising that point in response to Wilson, he used a tactic that had been proving very effective — he quoted the words of Wilson himself, who had said on 5 March 1917 that the preservation of internal peace 'imposes upon each nation the duty of seeing to it that all influences proceeding from its own citizens meant to encourage or assist revolutions in other states should be sternly and effectively suppressed and prevented.'

Once the United States ratified the Covenant, de Valera argued, 'England will insist on America acting in the letter and spirit of that declaration. Disguise it as we may, the new Covenant is simply a new Holy Alliance.'

'Unless America makes an explicit reservation in the case of Ireland,' he continued, 'the ratification of the Covenant by America will mean that England can hold that America has inferentially decided against Ireland, has admitted England's claim to Ireland as part of her possessions, the integrity of which America must evermore lend her assistance in maintaining.'[40]

Later the Irish leader elaborated further by explaining that while he was not afraid American troops would be used directly against Ireland, he did think 'they would, if England demanded it, be used against other nations that might decide to assist Ireland — for example, against France, or Spain, or China, or Russia, or any other state or people that might on the grounds of humanity or other grounds, so decide.'[41]

Although de Valera did not openly question the sincerity of Wilson's intimation that the United States would support Ireland's claim to self-determination at the League, he did contend such support would be too late. Britain would simply kill any discussion of the matter by insisting that the Irish question was an internal British affair. As a result the proposed use of Article XI would be like trying to recover a horse after a robbery, rather than trying to prevent the theft in the first place.

'It is before the signing of the Covenant that those who are in sympathy with Ireland, those who do not want to be unjust to Ireland, must act, not afterwards,' de Valera argued. 'Instead of relying on Article XI to undo the wrong of Article X, why not set up Article X in such a form that there will be no wrong to be undone?'[42]

The answer to this question was that President Wilson was afraid that if the United States Senate attached reservations to the Covenant, other countries would adopt reservations of their own, which could lead to a fiasco. In order to elicit sufficient public support to pressurise senators to ratify the Versailles Treaty without any debilitating reservations Wilson embarked on his grand tour. That tour was barely three weeks old when it was suddenly suspended and the President returned to the capital. He had suffered a stroke, but his condition, which deteriorated appreciably after a second attack, was carefully concealed from the public. As he lay ill, the controversy over American ratification continued.

Imitating Wilson's tactics, de Valera set out from New York on 1 October 1919 on a whistle-stop tour of his own which was to bring him through some nineteen states in the following eight weeks. Most of the travelling was done by rail. At small towns he simply spoke to gatherings at the railroad station, often from the train itself. At major overnight stops he was frequently met by official deputations and taken through those cities as the focal point of a grand parade. During such stops he delivered up to six speeches.

Throughout the tour de Valera continued his efforts not only to identify the Irish cause with America's wartime goals but also to link the question of Irish recognition with his opposition to the Covenant. At a banquet in Philadelphia on his first evening, in fact, he emphasised his willingness to accept the Covenant if the Irish Republic were first recognised. 'If the Irish Republic is recognised,' he said, 'the Covenant will be acceptable.'[43] Without prior recognition, however, he contended that Article X would commit the United States to support perpetual British sovereignty over Ireland, which could lead to a situation in which Americans would be fighting to keep Ireland under British domination.

While raising the spectre of Americans fighting on Britain's behalf, de Valera ridiculed the suggestion that recognising the Irish Republic might lead to an Anglo-American conflict. 'You need not hesitate for fear that England will be offended,' he declared in Milwaukee. 'England dares not declare war on you, and you know it. She'd have to borrow the money from you with which to fight you. If America had insisted on her rights at Paris, she could have gained everything she asked.'[44]

In St Louis he dismissed the possibility of using Article XI as Wilson had intimated. 'If President Wilson was not sufficiently influential to get the Irish case before the Peace Conference, working in an unofficial way,' the Irish leader argued, 'he will not be influential enough to get the case of Ireland before the Council of the League of Nations.'[45]

If there were to be a proper covenant for a true league of all nations, de Valera repeatedly stressed the necessity of rectifying the situation which would be created by Article X with regard to the right of national self-determination. 'Article XI is the whole essence of the League,' he told a Denver gathering. 'It is the preserving clause. If you preserve the conditions with which you start, then start right. It is wrong to preserve wrong; that is why we are against the League of Nations.'[46]

While de Valera was touring the country Senator Thomas Walsh, a strong supporter of Wilson, tried to alleviate the opposition to the Covenant and shore up his own political position with his many Irish-American constituents by proposing a resolution in the United States Senate that would, in effect, have formalised Wilson's implied offer to use Article XI on Ireland's behalf. The Walsh resolution stipulated that on joining the world body, 'the United States should present to the Council or the Assembly of the League the state of affairs in Ireland, and the right of its people to self-determination.' But nothing ever came of the resolution, which was undermined when Walsh admitted that the League would be unable to act if Britain insisted that the Irish question was purely a British domestic issue.[47] As a result the resolution was never even voted on, but the Senate did adopt fourteen reservations to the Versailles Treaty, including one to Article X of the Covenant. When it came to voting on the treaty with the reservations, however, Wilson's supporters joined with irreconcilable opponents to defeat the agreement on 26 November 1919.

Having heard the news in southern California, de Valera cancelled the remainder of his tour, which was to have brought him through the southern states, and he returned directly to New York. He had secured neither American recognition nor an American commitment to support Ireland's case at the League of Nations, but he had at least contributed towards the rejection of the Covenant, although his contribution and that of the Irish-Americans was greatly exaggerated at the time.

The question of American membership of the League had suffered a serious setback, but Wilson's supporters worked hard to get the matter reconsidered. The treaty was again brought before the Senate in March 1920 when two further reservations were adopted. One of these actually referred to Ireland:

> In consenting to the ratification of the Treaty with Germany, the United States adheres to the principle of self-determination and the resolution of sympathy with the expectations of the Irish people for a government of their own choice, adopted by the Senate on June 6th, 1919, and declares that when such government is attained by Ireland, a consummation it is hoped is at hand, it should promptly be admitted as a member of the League of Nations.

The reservation, which was passed by thirty-eight votes to thirty-six, would virtually commit the representatives of the United States to support Irish membership, if America entered the League of Nations. As a result de Valera was estatic. He sent Griffith an open telegram describing the resolution as a victory for Ireland: 'Our mission has been successful. The principle of self-determination has been formally adopted in an international instrument. Ireland has been given her place amongst the nations by the greatest nation of them all.'[48]

Privately the Irish leader admitted that he had achieved his goal. The reservation was, he wrote, 'what I had been always wishing for, and it came finally beyond expectations.'[49] This jubilation was indicative of de Valera's inexperience in American politics, because he obviously did not recognise that the resolution had been passed only as a tactical means of making the reservations so unpalatable to ensure the defeat of the actual treaty. Indeed sixteen of the thirty-eight senators who had called for the reservation had no intention of voting for the treaty itself.[50]

When the treaty with its sixteen reservations came up for a final Senate vote, two days later, Wilson's supporters again joined with his diehard critics to kill the agreement. As a result the United States never did become a member of the League of Nations.

CHAPTER TWO

# Not Enough Room for the Judge

## *The Irish Split in America*

Although the rejection of the Versailles Treaty by the United States Senate closed one avenue by which de Valera had hoped to gain recognition, another was opened in December 1919 when Congressman William Mason of Illinois introduced a bill in the House of Representatives to allocate money for salaries of American diplomatic representatives to Ireland. This was a roundabout step to secure recognition, which would normally be accorded by the White House with Congress signifying its approval by allocating funds for the mission. The process was simply being reversed in the case of the Mason Bill, with the result that the enactment of the legislation would be tantamount to formal Congressional recognition, but the proposal ran into stout opposition.

One of the strongest arguments against it was that it would be an act of treachery against America's ally in the recent war — Britain. Many people felt the British needed to hold on to Ireland for self-preservation because of the danger that an independent Ireland would align with Britain's enemies in order to get revenge for the centuries of misrule. Congressman Tom Connolly of Texas contended, for instance, that the British could never permit Ireland to become independent because she would 'become the prey of every scheming nation in Europe.'[1]

De Valera tried to counter this argument in New York the following weekend by demonstrating that Irish independence could be made compatible with Britain's security. He suggested Britain should offer a treaty to Ireland on the lines of the 1901 treaty between the United States and Cuba, in accordance with which the latter gave an assurance that she would never allow her independence to be compromised. The press, however, paid little attention until he repeated those views to a correspondent of the *Westminster Gazette* a few days later.

In the course of the interview de Valera explained there were four ways of ensuring Britain's security without interfering with Ireland's independence. One, there could be an international guarantee of Ireland's neutrality as in the case of Belgium, or two, 'in a genuine League of Nations the contracting parties could easily by mutual compact bind themselves to respect and defend the integrity and national independence of each other, and guarantee it by the strength of the whole.'²

The other two methods of guaranteeing that Irish independence would not endanger Britain's security had distinct American parallels. De Valera suggested the London government could simply declare a doctrine for the British Isles similar to the Monroe Doctrine used by the United States to insist against European encroachment on the independence of Latin American countries. The fourth proposal was for Britain to agree to a treaty similar to the treaty between the United States and Cuba. The Americans had protected their interests then, the Irish leader said, by demanding that the Cuban government promise it would 'never enter into any treaty or other compact with any foreign power or powers which shall impair or tend to impair Cuban independence, nor in any manner authorise or permit any foreign power or powers to obtain by colonisation or for military or naval purposes or otherwise, lodgment in or control over any portion of the said island.'

'Why doesn't Britain do with Ireland as the United States did with Cuba?' de Valera asked. 'Why doesn't Britain declare a Monroe Doctrine for her neighbouring island? The people of Ireland, so far from objecting, would co-operate with their whole soul.'

In advocating the Cuban analogy de Valera had quoted from the first clause of what was known as the Platt Amendment, which had been incorporated into the 1901 treaty with Cuba. He did not make any reference to other Platt clauses demanding that the United States should be granted naval and coaling stations in Cuba in addition to the right to intervene there for the preservation of the island's independence.

De Valera did not really intend for the other clauses of the Platt Amendment to be part of his proposal. In fact, he actually intimated during the interview that he would not be in favour of allowing Britain to have Irish bases. In summarising his arguments, he complained 'it is not her national safety nor her legitimate security that England wants to safeguard. By any of the four methods indicated she could have made provision for these. What she wants to make provision for, I repeat, is the perpetuation of her domination of the seas by her control of the great Irish harbours.'

Unknown to de Valera there was an arrangement between the *Westminster Gazette* and the New York *Globe* to share their material, so the interview appeared on the front page of the New York newspaper next day. In its report, headlined 'Compromise Suggested by Irish', the *Globe* mentioned that the salient features of the interview were de Valera's call for 'the granting of complete independence to Ireland on the same basis as the independence granted to Cuba' and 'under the operation of a policy based on the American Monroe Doctrine.' The report made no suggestion that the Irish leader was prepared to accept less than 'complete independence'.[3]

He had achieved part of his objective. In an editorial in the same edition, the *Globe* observed that de Valera had offered 'a really convincing assurance' to 'the seemingly unanswerable argument that Irish independence' would be extremely damaging to Britain's security. The editorial concluded, however, that the assurance in question actually introduced 'a new principle. It is a withdrawal by the official head of the Irish Republic of the demand that Ireland be set free to decide her own international relations.'

Although the Philadelphia *Irish Press* and the New York *Irish World* both welcomed de Valera's initiative, the *Gaelic American* condemned the proposals as an offer of surrender to Britain, and the *Globe* editorial was cited to back up the charge.

De Valera quickly clarified that he had only quoted the

one clause from the Platt Amendment and that he was referring to it alone when he put foward the Cuban analogy. He had no hesitation in reaffirming that Ireland would give Britain 'the guarantee that is contained in the first article of the Platt Amendment.'[4] This would not be incompatible with Irish independence on which, he emphasised, he had no intention of compromising.

Notwithstanding the Irish leader's convincing clarification of the interview, the *Gaelic American* continued to be critical of the use of the Cuban analogy. The editor, John Devoy, contended that it was not possible to divorce the first clause from the remainder. 'When a part of a document is offered in evidence in court, or in negotiations,' he wrote, 'the whole document becomes subject for consideration.'[5]

Devoy was obviously spoiling for a fight because de Valera had been aligning himself with a rival faction within Clan-na-Gael, the American affiliate of the Irish Republican Brotherhood (IRB). Although the Irish President was accused of causing a bitter split within Irish-American ranks with his *Westminster Gazette* interview, the split had been developing before he ever came to the United States. Indeed, Irish-American politics had been faction-riddled for decades and it would have been most surprising if the apparent unity that existed upon his arrival had lasted very long.

There were already two contending factions within Clan-na-Gael, which controlled FOIF in much the same way as the IRB had controlled the Irish Volunteers before the Easter Rebellion. Judge Daniel Cohalan of the New York Supreme Court and John Devoy were themselves in effective control of Clan-na-Gael, but there was a rival faction in Philadelphia led by Tyrone-born Joseph McGarrity, the proprietor of the *Irish Press,* and the newspaper's editor — another Tyrone man — Patrick McCartan, who had gone to the United States as an envoy of the IRB. They were critical that FOIF was devoting more attention to American politics than to Irish affairs. As a result men whose prime loyalty was to the Irish cause tended to gravitate to McGarrity, who complained that too much of the money being collected by FOIF — only twenty-five per cent of which was earmarked for Ireland — was being spent in the United States on such things as opposition to the League of Nations. The McGarrity faction also accused Cohalan and Devoy of not working hard enough for official American recognition of the Irish Republic.

There can be little doubt that Cohalan and his supporters were primarily interested in essentially American goals, such as keeping the United States out of the League of Nations and weakening British influence in America. They made no secret of this fact, but they were also anxious to assist the Irish struggle for independence, if only to satiate their own anglophobia by weakening Britain. From the American standpoint it seemed to them that the best way of getting favourable action was not by calling for recognition of the Irish Republic, but by exploiting the slogan of self-determination for small nations, which Wilson had led the American people to believe was one of the principal reasons for their involvement in the First World War. 'The term self-determination has caught them and holding it constantly up to him is the best means of getting him to do something,' Devoy wrote. 'Recognition of the Irish Republic he could easily refuse, but making good his oft quoted phrase is something of a different kind.'[6]

In addition to using slogans with which the American people could readily identify, Cohalan also believed that it was important that FOIF should be free from any taint of alien dictation. Thus when the Irish leader tried 'to be let into the political steps' being planned by the judge, the latter made it clear that he did not want de Valera 'to go near the political end at all.'[7] This led to difficulties.

'The trouble is purely one of personalities,' de Valera wrote. 'I cannot feel confidence enough in a certain man to let him have implicit control of tactics here without consultation and agreement with me.'[8]

The problem therefore really centered around who was going to determine the policy which would be used in the United States to secure American support for the Irish cause. De Valera felt that he was entitled to have the final say on policy formulation, although he was prepared to consult with the Irish-Americans. 'On the ways and means they have to be consulted,' he wrote, 'but I reserve the right to use my judgment as to whether any means suggested is or is not in conformity with our purpose.'[9]

In short, de Valera was insisting on having the last word on tactics to be used by Irish-Americans, while Cohalan wanted him to have no say at all in such matters. A clash between them was therefore virtually inevitable. In fact, there were difficulties between them from their very first meeting.

'I realised early,' de Valera wrote, that 'big as this country is it was not big enough to hold the judge and myself.'[10] Irish interests were only of secondary consideration to Cohalan, while de Valera wanted Irish considerations to be paramount. 'I desired that Ireland's interests should come first,' the Irish President wrote. 'I held that the I[rish]here were organised not in their own interests here so much as to help Ireland. I held that the money contributed was obtained in the belief that it would be used as directly as possible for Ireland.'[11]

'It is sympathy for Ireland that has enabled such an organisation as the FRIENDS OF IRISH FREEDOM to be built up,' de Valera wrote on another occasion. 'That is why the vast mass of the rank and file have joined — that is why they have contributed, and I will not allow myself to be in any hobble skirts with respect to the doings of anything which we feel certain is for the good of the Cause.'[12]

The first clash with Cohalan occurred over de Valera's plan to raise money for the Irish cause by selling republican bonds in the United States. On the one hand, the judge was opposed to any fund-raising which would interfere with the drive launched in February by FOIF to collect a million dollars, but he also noted that until the Irish Republic had been officially recognised by the United States, the sale of such bonds would be illegal.

Those difficulties were overcome by simply waiting until after FOIF wound up its fund-raising campaign at the end of August 1919. In return, the organisation underwrote the launching of a drive to sell, not bonds, but bond-certificates entitling purchasers to buy actual bonds of similar value when the Irish Republic was officially recognised. By this subtle arrangement the legal complications were overcome. Once the scheme had been thought out by a committee including Cohalan, de Valera personally secured independent legal advice on its feasibility from the future President, Franklin D. Roosevelt, who was a junior partner in a New York law firm at the time.

Although Cohalan and de Valera co-operated on arrangements for launching the bond-certificates, this did little to alleviate the growing tension between them. The former was annoyed that de Valera was interfering in American affairs, while de Valera thought that the judge was not only trying to dictate policy on essentially Irish matters, but was also using the Irish question to serve narrow American ends. As Cohalan was a highly partisan politician who had abandoned the Democratic Party to join the Republican opposition over a long-standing feud with President Wilson, the Irish leader was very wary about being caught up in the judge's political schemes.

In the summer of 1919, de Valera refused to go along blindly with efforts to arrange for him to address the United States Congress. Cohalan had approached Senator William E. Borah of the Senate Foreign Relations Committee with a view to making arrangements for such a Congressional appearance. But, as Borah was an isolationist Republican and a strong critic of Wilson, the Irish leader insisted that the approach to Congress should be bi-partisan, with the result that a Democratic supporter of the American President, Senator James D. Phelan of California, who had backed the various Irish resolutions, was asked to co-sponsor the Congressional approach. De Valera, Borah, Phelan, and Cohalan subsequently met to discuss the matter, but nothing ever came of their efforts, which left the judge convinced that there would have been a much better chance of success had Borah been allowed to handle things in his own way.

There was really a certain amount of justification in the complaints Cohalan and de Valera had about each other. The Irish leader had unquestionably intervened in the affairs of the United States by advising the American people to take a reservationist position in the controversy over the League of Nations. In a report to the cabinet in Dublin, he admitted that he was trying to let Wilson know that 'Irishmen and men and women of Irish blood' would support a revised Covenant.[13]

'I have tried to get it conveyed to the President,' he wrote on another occasion 'that all would back [a] genuine attempt to found a real league of nations.'[14] As has already been shown, his criterion for such a league was simply that it should include Ireland. Thus de Valera was actually indicating that Irish-Americans would support the League of Nations, if provisions were made for Ireland's membership. He took that stand although FOIF leaders had made it clear that they would be opposed to American membership of the League even if it guaranteed Irish freedom.

Men like Cohalan were motivated by traditional American isolationism. They despised Wilson's brand of internationalism, and they therefore resented de Valera's blatant attempt to assume the role of spokesman for Irish-Americans in espousing what was outright Wilsonian internationalism. In fairness to the Irish leader, it should be pointed out that he was trying to steer a non-partisan course between Democrats loyal to Wilson and Republicans opposed to him — in other words, between those who wanted the Covenant as it was written and those who wished to destroy it. In short, he was trying to reconcile the irreconcilable, which annoyed irreconcilables like Cohalan and Devoy.

During the controversy over the *Westminster Gazette* interview, de Valera had the startling audacity to complain that the continuing criticism in the *Gaelic American* might damage his plans to use American opinion. In an extraordinary letter to Cohalan on 20 February 1920, he freely admitted that he planned to use 'the great lever of American public opinion' as a wedge to achieve his aims in the United States. Since the Irish-Americans were to be the pointed end of this metaphorical lever, he was therefore anxious to satisfy himself that the metal at the end was of the right temper. 'The articles of the *Gaelic American* and certain incidents that have resulted from them, give me grounds for fear that in a moment of stress, the point of the lever would fail me,' he wrote. 'I am led to understand that these articles in the *Gaelic American* have your consent and approval. Is this so?' He added that 'it is vital that I know exactly how you stand in the matter.'

Cohalan replied disclaiming any responsibility for Devoy's views but nevertheless agreeing with the criticism expressed in the *Gaelic American*, because he contended that 'a British Monroe Doctrine that would make Ireland an ally of England, and thus buttress the falling British Empire so as to further oppress India and Egypt and other subject lands would be so immoral and so utterly at variance with the ideals and traditions of the Irish people as to make it indefensible to them as it would be intolerable to the liberty-loving people of the world.' The judge emphasised in addition that he had no intention of allowing himself to be used as part of a political lever to achieve Irish ends. He had, he wrote, always acted 'as an American, whose only allegiance is to America, and as one to whom the interest and security of my country are to be preferred to those of any and all other lands.'[15] Consequently he was not about to let himself be used by any alien representative, and he warned that de Valera was in danger of making a serious mistake in trying to use Americans for what were essentially alien ends.

'Do you really think for a moment that American public opinion will permit any citizen of another country to interfere, as you suggest, in American affairs?' Cohalan asked. 'Do you think that any self-respecting American will permit himself to be used in such a manner by you? If so, I may assure you that you are woefully out of touch with the spirit of the country in which you are sojourning.'[16]

De Valera was indeed a novice as far as American politics were concerned, which became only too evident with his reaction to the adoption of the reservation relating to Ireland while the United States Senate was reconsidering the Versailles Treaty in March 1920. He did not recognise that many of those who had supported the reservation had done so simply to ensure the defeat of the treaty.

On the same day that the Senate rejected the treaty,

Cohalan complained to a meeting of some seventy-five prominent Irish-Americans in New York City that even though the Irish leader knew very little about American politics, he consulted no one and had by his arrogance alienated people who had spent a lifetime helping the Irish cause. In the course of a tirade lasting about half an hour, the judge accused de Valera of not only interfering in American affairs and causing 'considerable friction' among Irish-Americans but also with offering 'a compromise to England which would put Ireland in the position of accepting a protectorate from England, and consenting to an alliance with that country which would align the race with England as against the United States in the case of war.'[17] While there could be no question about the validity of the accusation that the Irish leader had interfered in American affairs to serve Irish ends, Cohalan's own remarks left little doubt that the judge was himself interfering in Irish affairs to serve American ends.

At the insistence of Joe McGarrity, de Valera was invited to explain his position to the meeting. There followed some heated exchanges during which the Irish leader tactlessly blurted out that he was not in the country a month when he realised that America was not big enough for himself and the judge. Bishop William Turner of Buffalo thereupon observed that Cohalan could hardly be expected 'to leave his native land just because the President had decided to come.' After some ten hours of often bitter recrimination the bishop eventually persuaded the two sides to declare a truce, and the meeting broke up on the understanding that de Valera would not henceforth interfere in purely American affairs, while Cohalan and his people would keep out of essentially Irish affairs.[18]

Although de Valera was supposed to keep out of American affairs, he obviously never really intended to do so. This was evident from a letter he wrote to Griffith less than a week after the New York meeting, in which he made some political observations clearly showing that he had no intention of upholding his end of the understanding. He actually suggested that the Dáil should 'secretly' authorise him to spend between a quarter and a half million dollars on political activities in the United States during the 1920 election campaign. He was anxious to keep the matter secret in order to avoid further trouble for as long as possible with the Cohalan-Devoy faction, so as not to upset the Bond-certificate Drive, which had been launched in January 1920. 'It is very important,' he wrote, 'that there should not be an open rupture until the Bond Drive were over at any rate.'[19]

De Valera was hoping to use the votes of Irish-Americans to secure political support for the Irish cause. He realised the whole question of recognition rested with the White House, and it was obvious that 'the most, under any circumstances, one could hope to get is a friendly President,' but, he added, 'I don't believe that even a friendly President, except under international conditions very different from the present, would go to the length of giving us formal recognition.' He thought this would only happen if Anglo-American relations deteriorated to the extent where 'America might wish for its own purposes to use the Irish situation as a weapon against Britain.'[20]

While the immediate prospects of an Anglo-American rift were remote, de Valera felt there was still another way of gaining recognition — by providing a Presidential candidate with Irish-American support in return for a firm public commitment on the Irish recognition issue. If such a candidate were elected President, he then would be committed to recognising the Irish Republic.

Although Irish-Americans constituted a distinct minority in the United States, they possessed political influence far in excess of their numbers. This was mainly due to two factors. Firstly, they tended to block vote as directed by their own political leaders, and secondly, they were concentrated in the large urban areas of the most populous states.

In New York, the state with the largest number of electoral votes for the Presidency, the Irish were concentrated in the New York City area, where their support was crucial to any Democratic candidate, as upstate New York was heavily Republican. Thus, the Democratic candidate had to win well in New York City to carry the state, and it was highly improbable that any Democrate could secure sufficient votes to win the state without the support of the Irish-American community. As the so-called 'Irish vote' tended to have the same kind of pivotal influence in other important states, the Irish-Americans had an inordinate influence within the Democratic Party.

De Valera hoped to use that influence to further the recognition cause. 'The Democrats will bid high for the Irish vote now,' he explained to Griffith. 'Without it they have not the slightest chance of winning at the elections unless something extraordinary turns up.' But 'with the Irish vote,' he believed that 'the Democrats might still win.'[21]

While anxious to win the support of the Democratic Party, de Valera had by no means written off the Republicans. 'Our policy here has always been to be as friendly with one of the political parties as with the other,' he wrote. If the Irish-American vote was important to the Democrats, then it would be twice as valuable to the Republicans, because solid Irish-American backing could virtually guarantee the election of a Republican Presidential candidate, as it would not only deprive the Democratic nominee of a vital part of his party's traditional support but would compel him to obtain twice as much independent support from elsewhere to make up for the defections of the Irish-Americans. Consequently de Valera was optimistic about the possibility of being able to use a Republican candidate.

He thought that Senator Hiram Johnson, a Republican from California, was probably 'the best man available'. He tried to get Johnson to make a firm public commitment on the Irish recognition issue. 'I had been for a long time urging Johnson's friends, also friends of ours, to get him to make such a declaration in order that our people could start working for him.' de Valera wrote.

The Irish leader believed that securing a firm commitment in advance was 'the only way to play the cards for Ireland', but John Devoy in the *Gaelic American* gratuitously endorsed Johnson, which undermined the whole scheme. 'He has gained his point now I see — we have lost ours,' de Valera wrote. 'However, it may come all right, though it is disappointing to see a clear nap hand played poorly.'[22]

'Sometimes,' he added, 'when I see the strategic position which the Irish here occupy in American politics I feel like crying when I realise what could be made of it if there was real genuine team work *for Ireland alone* being done. As far as politics is concerned, the position is almost everything one could wish for.'

De Valera seemed peculiarly unable to understand that the Irish-Americans considered themselves as primarily Americans and their 'Irish' prefix was indicative only of their ancestry, not their allegiance. To have engaged in what he described as 'real genuine team work *for Ireland alone*' would have meant subordinating American interests to those of Ireland. He was actually thinking about Americans being prepared to vote for their President simply in terms of what that man would do for Ireland, which seemed to confirm Cohalan's assessment of the Irish leader being 'woefully out of touch with the spirit' of the American people.

When the Mason Bill to allocate funds for a diplomatic mission to Ireland ran into such stout opposition that it was found necessary to abandon it, de Valera drafted a substitute resolution in accordance with which Congress would declare that as the Irish people had democratically established an independent republic, the President of the United States should act in accordance with 'the principle of national self-determination' and give 'official recognition to that Republic and its duly elected Government.' The Foreign Affairs Committee of the House of Representatives rejected the resolution. The committee did eventually accept a considerably modified resolution merely calling on Congress 'to express its sympathy with the aspiration of the Irish people for a government of their own choice.' That resolution was subsequently killed by the hostility of the committee's chairman, who prevented the motion from getting to the floor of the House.

The campaign for recognition had thus received a serious setback, but de Valera did not despair. He had plans to expand the recognition campaign. He sent Harry Boland home to Dublin to get the Dáil's authorisation for a broad international plan, which Boland explained to the Dáil cabinet in June 1920. The President wanted to be authorised to appoint consular and diplomatic agents to such countries as the Soviet Union, France, Spain, Italy, Austria, Germany, Denmark and Switzerland, with four new agents to be appointed to the United States to serve in Boston, Chicago, New Orleans, and San Francisco.[23]

The suggested appointment of four further agents to the United States underscored the President's intention of having America play a vital role in that campaign. In fact, since the Dublin regime was having difficulties in communicating with the outside world, he actually envisaged using the American capital as a centre for co-ordinating the international activites of all the Irish foreign representatives. He even suggested that Robert Brennan, the director of propaganda, should be sent to the United States, where he would be charged with supplying propaganda material to the various diplomatic agents, who would be appointed by the President himself from a list of thirty names submitted by the Dáil. These agents would then report to both Washington, D.C., and Dublin.

De Valera also asked for authorisation to spend up to one million dollars on the recognition campaign, in addition to his earlier suggestion that up to half a million dollars be allocated to him for the American elections. As if to further emphasise the propagandist nature of the overall plan, he requested that Erskine Childers, the editor of the *Irish Bulletin* — the revolutionary regime's official organ — be appointed ambassador to the United States.

Members of the cabinet were on the whole in sympathy with the President's overall plan. They endorsed the monetary provisions, approved the appointment of new foreign representatives, and agreed that these agents should be directed from Washingon. The cabinent, however, rejected the request that Brennan and Childers be sent to America on the grounds that they were too valuable at home to be spared. It nevertheless obviously shared the President's views on the importance of the American role in the recognition campaign, as it advised him to remain in the United States to press the recognition case, which the ministry believed should be formally presented in

Washington before demands were made on any other countries.[24]

The President's efforts to secure official American recognition, however, again brought him into conflict with the Cohalan-Devoy faction. In June 1920 the political truce collapsed after de Valera went to Chicago for the Republican Party's National Convention, where he hoped to influence the Republicans to adopt a plank calling for recognition of the Irish Republic in the party's election platform.

Believing that these efforts could hamper FOIF plans to influence the convention, Cohalan got Michael J. Gallagher, the Roman Catholic Bishop of Detroit, to try to persuade the President to leave Chicago. The bishop met de Valera and informed him of FOIF plans and explained that alien interference could be counter-productive.[25]

According to the bishop, Cohalan did not intend to ask for outright recognition of the Irish Republic, because he feared that even in the unlikely event of the Republicans adopting such a position, the candidate standing on that plank would probably be defeated in the November elections. Such a candidate, he explained, would incur the wrath of the anglophile press, which would lead the electorate to conclude that official American recognition would cause serious difficulties, possibly even war, between the United States and Britain. In addition, if a candidate were elected on a platform which included a recognition plank, this would not necessarily mean that Ireland would get that recognition.

The fulfilment of the plank would actually depend on the President himself. In 1912, Woodrow Wilson had been elected on a platform with a plank advocating that an individual be eligible for only one term as President, but Wilson himself ignored it and ran for re-election in 1916. Moreover, in the latter election he had stressed his determination to keep the United States out of the First World War, but he was not even a month into his second term when he asked Congress for a declaration of war. Such events convinced Cohalan that it was more important to help the right man win the party's nomination than to get a strong plank accepted.

The judge, who was supporting Senator Hiram Johnson, believed if the latter were nominated, he would be elected and would appoint Senator Borah, a staunch supporter of the Irish cause, as Secretary of State. When Bishop Gallagher outlined this scenario, de Valera rejected the plan. He explained he could not put such trust in Senator Johnson, or any other individual for that matter. Regardless of who became the next President of the United States, even if it were to be Cohalan himself, de Valera said, that individual would not accord recognition to the Irish Republic unless first convinced that American public opinion would sustain him. Thus, if Johnson were elected, and Cohalan was right about public opinion being opposed to recognising the Dublin government, Ireland would not get that recognition.

'For the Chief Executive of a nation to take the step of according the recognition we seek, he would naturally want to feel assured that public opinion was behind him,' de Valera said. 'On us lies the duty of securing that opinion, and when it is secured, of making it manifest to all.' He added that 'agitation of this question at the great political conventions in the most public manner possible, and the effort to secure in all of them a plank in favour of recognition was the greatest step forward we could take towards securing what we need.'[26]

Rejecting the advice not to interfere at the convention, de Valera went ahead with his own plans. The Irish mission opened offices across from the convention centre and published a daily newsletter. On the eve of the convention they organised a torch-light parade involving some 5,000 marchers, who were afterwards addressed by de Valera. 'The Republicans must promise to recognise the Irish Republic,' he told them. 'All of Chicago wants this — I know the entire country wants this — I have been all over the country and I know.'[27]

'There was no chance of offending America that we did not take,' according to McCartan. The Irish actions were so glaring that the Chicago *Daily Tribune* carried a cartoon of the Irish leader with the comment: 'De Valera is not really a candidate in this Convention'.[28] When de Valera tried to get a personal hearing before the party's subcommittee on resolutions, he was refused and his plank calling for official recognition was heavily defeated in committee by a vote of twelve-to-one.

Later, with no little difficulty, Cohalan managed to persuade the subcommittee to adopt, by seven votes to six, a proposal calling for 'recognition of the principle that the people of Ireland have a right to determine freely, without dictation from outside, their own government institutions and their international relations with other states and people.' But on learning of the acceptance of the Cohalan plank de Valera objected to it and demanded that it be withdrawn. The chairman of the subcommittee on resolutions was so annoyed at this foreign intervention that he reversed his vote and killed the plank.

Afterwards de Valera issued a statement to the effect that he had taken his stand because the Cohalan resolution was too vague. 'I believe,' he said, 'it was positively harmful to our interests that a resolution misrepresenting Ireland's claim by understating it should have been presented.'[29] In the end he secured nothing, save possibly the undying enmity of Cohalan and Devoy.

The *Gaelic American* was strongly critical of de Valera's actions in undermining Cohalan's plank. Had the Republican Party adopted the judge's plank, Devoy believed that the Democrats would have then been tempted to go at least that far. When de Valera went to San Francisco for the Democratic Party's National Convention, he was again unsuccessful. His recognition proposal was defeated on the floor of the convention, which led to renewed criticism of his actions in Chicago.

Was Cohalan's proposal really an understatement of Ireland's claim, as de Valera contended?

It is noteworthy that the Chicago *Daily Tribune*, which had been very sympathetic towards the Irish cause, subsequently carried an editorial strongly critical of the Cohalan plank on the grounds that it could have led to serious difficulties — even war — with Britain, because it 'was in effect a recognition of the secession of Ireland from the British Empire and its recognition as an independent state.'[30] De Valera's contention, on the other hand, that the plank understated Ireland's claim was based on the fact that it called, not for recognition of the Irish Republic, but only for recognition of the principle that the Irish people had a right to self-determination.

Although de Valera frequently contended that eighty per cent of Irish voters supported the establishment of the Irish Republic, his figure was grossly inflated. It had apparently been arrived at by lumping all the people together who did not vote for Unionist candidates. Although Sinn Féin — the only party to stand on a republican platform — did win almost seventy per cent of the Irish seats in the general election of 1918, it secured only 47.7 per cent of the popular vote, which was short of even a majority.[31] Thus, if it were only on that point alone, Cohalan would have been justified in simply calling for self-determination, rather than for outright recognition of a government which did not formally have the support of a majority of the Irish people.

The Irish leader was obviously less than candid when he released his statement about the Cohalan plank. Before going to the United States he had stressed that Ireland was seeking only the right of self-determination. Then upon his arrival in New York, when McCartan complained that Cohalan had reduced the Irish Republican claim to one of mere self-determination, the President replied that the self-determination approach was a good policy.[32] He subsequently emphasised that point by dwelling on it in many of his American speeches.

'What I seek in America,' he said on more than one occasion, 'is that the United States recognise in Ireland's case Ireland's right to national self-determination, that and nothing more.'[33] Following his return to Ireland at the end of the year, he again emphasised the same theme when he told a Swiss correspondent in May 1921 'the principle for which we are fighting is the principle of Ireland's right to complete self-determination.'[34]

De Valera's real reason for undermining the Cohalan resolution was not because it understated Ireland's claim. Rather, he wanted to demonstrate that he, as Irish leader, was determining all policy relating to Ireland. He did not want anyone to think that he had 'become a puppet to be manipulated' by the judge. A few months earlier, he had reported to the cabinet in Dublin that he did not want American politicians to get the idea that Cohalan was 'the real power behind our movement — the man to whom they would have to go. Were I [to] allow myself to appear thus as a puppet, apart from any personal pride, the movement would suffer a severe blow. Those who had held aloof because of the plea that the Judge is running this movement would cry out that they were justified.'[35] If the Irish-Americans wished to help Ireland, de Valera was determined that he should himself determine what form their help should take. He subsequently explained to a private session of the Dáil that his differences with the Cohalan-Devoy faction centred around his resolve to make it 'impossible for individuals in America to use the name of Ireland for any purpose but the one Ireland wanted.'[36]

Following the Chicago debacle there were efforts to convene a conference to stop the feuding, and it was noteworthy that there was a move within the McGarrity faction to exclude de Valera himself. McCartan wrote at the time that the President tended to come to conferences without knowing exactly what he wanted yet seemed to have 'an unconscious contempt' for the opinions of others:

> The Chief presides and does all the talking. Has a habit of getting on to side issues and shutting off people who wish to speak and thus makes a bad impression if not sometimes enemies. Tends to force his own opinions without hearing from the other fellows and thus thinks he has co-operation when he only gets silent acquiescence.[37]

De Valera wanted a conference, too, but his aim was to re-organise Irish-Americans in order to make Irish recognition a campaign issue in the forthcoming American elections, especially the Presidential election. In a letter to Bishop Gallagher, who was elected President of FOIF shortly after the Chicago convention, he suggested that a Race Convention should be convened at some central point like Chicago in order to make arrangements for a fresh campaign. He candidly admitted that he was anxious that America's 'official policy towards Ireland should come forward definitely, explicitly and above board during the coming election campaign.'[38]

By suggesting Chicago as the site for the convention, however, de Valera was obviously trying to break the stranglehold that the Cohalanites (most of whom were based in the New York area) had on FOIF. Their resentment over Irish interference in American affairs — already very strong — was further fuelled within a week by the public revelation that the Dáil had authorised de Valera to spend a half-a-million dollars on the forthcoming American elections. The President tried to take the harm out of the revelation by issuing a statement emphasising that it was misleading to speak of funds being for the American elections. 'In public and in private I have been scrupulously careful to avoid even appearing to take sides in the party politics of this country,' he declared. 'Apart from any possible illegality, it would obviously be bad taste on my part and most inexpedient.'[39]

De Valera seemed to think he was staying above party politics by being prepared to back sympathetic candidates without regard to their party affiliation, but it was patently absurd to contend, as did his authorised biographers, that he 'could never be accused of interference with American internal politics.'[40] Whether the United States should decide to join the League of Nations had certainly been an internal consideration, and de Valera privately acknowledged that in a letter to Griffith on 25 March 1920. 'The fight for the League of Nations,' he wrote, 'was purely an American affair attacked from a purely American angle, with advantages mainly for America.' Providing support for candidates in American elections would also have constituted an intervention in internal politics, and if de Valera really believed otherwise, then his capacity for self-deception was surely stupendous.

The Cohalanites were not deceived and their refusal to call another Race Convention before the November elections was understandable, if only on those grounds alone. They had other grounds, however. They were not prepared to facilitate what Devoy believed was an effort to remove them in order that de Valera would be able 'to show that nobody in America amounts to anything and that he is the kingpin of the movement.'[41]

FOIF leaders did agree to convene a National Council meeting of the organisation in New York on 17 September 1920. In an effort to secure the broadest representation possible de Valera personally telegraphed each council member to attend. As a result delegates from as far away as California came, but it quickly became apparent that his efforts to re-organise FOIF were doomed. He therefore walked out of the meeting trailed by his supporters shouting, 'Follow the President.' Outside, he called on 'all those anxious to help the Irish Republic' to assist him in founding a new organisation.[42]

The following morning he told a gathering in the Waldorf Astoria that the new organisation should be under the democratic control of members throughout the country, instead of being run by a cabal in New York. 'We from Ireland simply ask this:' de Valera said, 'that we should be accepted as the interpreters of what the Irish people want — we are responsible to them, they can repudiate us if we represent them incorrectly.'[43]

During the following weeks while preparations were being made to launch the new organisation, the Irish question played virtually no role in the Presidential election campaign. Irish-American resentment towards the Democratic President was so strong that there was a noticeable move towards the Republican candidate, Senator Warren G. Harding, who made no effort to woo voters on the Irish question. When asked during the campaign about his attitude towards the Irish issue, he simply replied: 'I would not care to undertake to say to Great Britain what she must do any more than I would permit her to tell us what we must do with the Phillipines.'[44]

In the week before the election de Valera finally sent his long delayed formal appeal to President Wilson asking for American recognition, but the manoeuvre, which was only a propaganda exercise, received little publicity outside Irish-American circles. The crusading ardour of the American people had obviously suffered during the three and a half years since Wilson led the country into the war with the avowed aim of making the world safe for democracy. Now the people were looking to get 'back to normalcy', and Harding won easily with that slogan.

With Harding's victory all hope of securing American recognition effectively vanished, and it became necessary to turn elsewhere. The only country which had shown any real interest in recognising the Irish Republic had been the Soviet Union, whose representatives in Washington had actually agreed to draft terms for a recognition treaty the previous summer, but de Valera had been afraid to authorise the formal conclusion of a treaty for fear that the establishment of diplomatic relations with the Bolshevik government might damage the possibility of securing official American recognition. His concern was shared by cabinet members in Dublin. 'They feel,' the cabinet secretary informed him, 'that a demand for recognition made to Russia *prior* to a similar demand being made in any other country might be availed of by British propagandists to misrepresent the Government of Ireland, and might militate against the success of such demands in other countries.'[45] The President therefore temporised but he did try to keep the Soviet representatives interested by secretly loaning their financially embarrassed mission in Washington some $20,000, and received in return some jewels as collateral.

After the presentation of the formal request for American recognition, Patrick McCartan was sent to the Soviet Union to revive the recognition negotiations, while de Valera remained in the United States to press ahead with plans for the establishment of the American Association for Recognition of the Irish Republic (AARIR), which was formally launched in Washington, D.C., on 16 November 1920. It prospered for some months and seemed to justify the President's belief that the leadership of the Cohalan-Devoy faction was unacceptable to many Irish-Americans. In the following year FOIF suffered serious defections as its membership declined to about 20,000 members, while AARIR's soared to about half a million people in the same period.

De Valera had intended to remain in America longer but changed his mind as a result of developments in Ireland. His American mission had been a qualified success. He had not achieved his primary aim of securing diplomatic recognition, nor had he helped to end the developing split among Irish-Americans, but he did leave behind a viable organisation that was primarily dedicated towards serving the Irish cause, rather than using the Irish situation to serve American ends. In addition, he collected over five million dollars and secured invaluable publicity for the independence movement at home. By his clever exploitation of the opportunities afforded for propaganda, he managed to exert enormous pressure on the British to negotiate an Irish settlement, if only to avoid Anglo-American difficulties.

CHAPTER THREE

# Dominion Status or the Status of a Dominion

*Negotiating with the British*

Whilst de Valera had given up hope of securing American recognition upon his return home, he still believed that American opinion could play an influential role in helping Ireland. In fact, he quickly proposed that the IRA should scale down its day-to-day activities and confront British forces instead in major monthly battles involving about five hundred men. In this way he believed the Irish struggle would receive maximum publicity and could be best exploited for propaganda purposes in the United States.[1]

British records reveal that Lloyd George was already concerned about American opinion in January 1921. He privately voiced disquiet over the effects his government's policy was having on Anglo-American relations. He told Bonar Law, the Conservative leader, that the British ambassador in Washington had 'given a most gloomy account' of the American situation. 'In the interests of peace with America,' the Prime Minister added, 'I think we ought to see de Valera and try to get a settlement.'[2] Bonar Law, who was in the influential position of having a virtual veto over government policy in view of his party's majority in parliament, killed the possibility of negotiations at that point.

Faced with British intransigence, de Valera intensified his efforts to enlist international support by establishing a Department of Foreign Affairs, the primary function of which was propaganda. On appointing Robert Brennan secretary of the department, for example, the President instructed him to keep in close touch with the Director of Propaganda. 'It is as much his department as yours,' de Valera wrote. 'It is in fact what I have called the "Statistical" or permanent-value-department of propaganda.'[3]

All the representatives the Dáil had sent abroad had been primarily engaged in propaganda, as their efforts to secure diplomatic recognition had been amounting to very little. Even the Soviet Union had lost the interest it had shown the previous summer. McCartan found upon his arrival in Russia that the Bolshevik authorities were more interested in securing a trade agreement with Britain. When such an agreement was signed in March 1921 it effectively killed any chance of Russian recognition. The Soviets did not want to antagonise Britain by recognising the Irish Republic.[4]

The desire to maintain friendly relations with Britain posed the most formidable barrier in the way of the Irish securing official recognition. In early 1921 there were rumours that the British had persuaded Pope Benedict XV to denounce the Irish republican regime. On 2 February 1921 de Valera wrote to Archbishop Patrick J. Hayes of New York in an effort to enlist his influence to forestall any such action by the Pope. 'I have,' the President wrote, 'what I must regard as sure information to the effect that the English have actually succeeded in impressing their views upon His Holiness and upon his advisers, and that His Holiness is on the point of issuing what will be regarded as a condemnation of those who are nobly striving in the cause of their country's liberty and freely offering their lives as a sacrifice.'[5]

Archbishop Hayes went to Rome and had talks on the question with Monsignor Sebastiani of the Vatican secretariat. It seemed that the Irish fears were well-founded, but the archbishop was obviously successful in rectifying the situation, because the Pope soon afterwards wrote to William Cardinal Logue with an assurance that he would pursue neutrality on the Irish question.[6]

Meanwhile de Valera was increasing the pressure on the British by deliberately portraying himself as a moderate not only in statements released to the press and in written answers to questions submitted by reporters, but also in a few instances during interviews granted to correspondents who were spirited blindfolded to his hiding place. As a result he received considerable international publicity and his carefully cultivated image as a moderate was thereby greatly enhanced.

With Lloyd George insisting that any settlement with Ireland would have to be on the lines of Dominion Home Rule, de Valera showed a deep interest in the whole dominion concept. He instructed Brennan to have the Department of Foreign Affairs 'pay particular attention' to the subject people of the British Empire and also the self-governing dominions. 'As regards the latter,' he wrote, 'all movements towards independence or towards a Federation in which the representatives of Great Britain would be on an equity with the other parts of the Empire should be noted.'[7]

The President indicated that the real status of the dominions would be acceptable to Ireland. Even a staunch imperialist like Bonar Law had admitted that the dominions had 'the right to decide their own destinies,' he explained. 'Thus the British dominions have had conceded to them all the rights that Irish republicans demand,' de Valera asserted. 'It is obvious that if these rights were not being denied to us we would not be engaged in the present struggle.' He went on to stress, as he had before, that Sinn Féin was not an isolationist movement. 'In fact,' he emphasised, 'we are thoroughly sane and reasonable people, not a coterie of political doctrinaires, or even party politicians, republican or other.'[8]

Before going to the United States de Valera had taken a rather hard line on the Ulster question. His message to the Unionists in the autumn of 1917 had been that they should abandon their allegiance to Britain or 'we will have to kick you out.'[9] A few months later during a speech in County Down he actually described the Unionists as 'a rock on the road' to Irish freedom, and he added that 'we must, if necessary, blast it out of our path.'[10] Upon his return from America, however, the Government of Ireland Act (1920), or the Partition Act as it was more popularly known, had already become law and he revealed a distinct softening in his attitude towards the Ulster problem by showing a willingness to accept a form of partition.

'There is plenty of room in Ireland for partition, real

partition and plenty of it,' he explained in one interview. The whole island, he suggested, should be parcelled up into administrative units associated in a confederation like Switzerland: 'If Belfast — or for that matter, all Carsonia as a unit — were a Swiss Canton like Berne, Geneva, or Zurich, it would have more control over its own affairs, economic, social and political, than it is given by the Westminster Partition Act. The real objection to that Act — prescinding from the question of its moral and political validity — is that it does not give Belfast and Ulster enough local liberty and power. In an Irish confederation they ought to get far more.'[11]

Although the President had apparently given a certain amount of consideration to the various forms of government, he proceeded in terms which suggested that he really did not understand the distinction between federal and confederate systems of government, as he used the two terms interchangeably. 'Incidentally,' he said immediately after referring to the Swiss model, 'this Federal scheme would not only solve the so-called Ulster question (apart from insoluble bigotry) but would provide the only proper *modus vivendi* between ports and cities like Cork and Dublin, agricultural areas like Meath, and industrial communities, such as Dublin; English-speaking districts like Clare, bilingual areas like Waterford, and Irish-speaking regions like Donegal or Connemara.'

De Valera went on to propose that in 'this federal system, whether dominion or republic', there could be a bicameral federal assembly, consisting of a national council with one representative elected per 20,000 population, and a council of counties with two deputies from each county. 'This Federal Assembly would deal only with such questions as concern Ireland as a whole (railways, customs, foreign relations, etc.), but owing to the autonomy of the counties would raise only a small Federal revenue — that of Switzerland is only about three millions. Moreover, the people of Ireland, and not this federal assembly would be sovereign.' To that end he proposed that eight counties or 30,000 voters could insist that any act of the Assembly be submitted to a direct vote of the people for ratification or rejection, and that about 50,000 people should be able to demand a referendum on proposals which, if accepted, would become law without ever passing through the assembly.

That de Valera suggested a federation or confederation seemed to imply his recognition that Northern Protestants did have some grounds for concern, but he showed little evidence that he personally appreciated the intensity of their fears. The outlined provisions for referenda seemed to conflict with the sectional rights that would supposedly be protected in a federal or confederate system, with the result that the proposal would not provide a guarantee to the minority against discrimination.

The President revealed a rather shallow perception of the depth of the Ulster problem. He seemed to think that the Unionists could easily be won over by economic measures. On the one hand, he actually advocated seeking from the Soviet Union favourable trade terms 'so as to use them as a lever to bring portions of the North — "Ulster" — to the side of the Republic.'[12] On the other hand, he was also ready to use the economic stick by supporting the Dáil's call for a boycott of goods produced in Belfast. He made it clear that he would even be prepared to intensify such pressure, which, of course, underscored the fears of Northerners by providing concrete proof of the kinds of discriminatory pressure the southern majority could exert. His stance on the whole boycott issue typified a superficial view of Unionist intransigence as something that would crumble with the onset of economic pressure from the rest of the island.

'When the elections come,' the President predicted in early March 1921, 'they will prove that industrial Ulster is not so blind to its own interests as to court being severed from its great market in the agricultural areas in the rest of the island. The boycott of Belfast goods which is now operating is but the opening stage of what will become a complete and absolute exclusion of Belfast goods if the Partition Act is put into effect.'[13]

Although de Valera seemed unable to appreciate the anxiety felt by Northern Protestants, he left little doubt about his willingness to accommodate the legitimate fears that Britain might have about the effects of Irish independence on her own national security. 'Time after time,' he emphasised, 'we have indicated that if England can show any right with which Ireland's right as a nation would clash, we are willing that these be adjusted by negotiations and treaty.'[14] He reinforced this the following month by stressing that Ireland would guarantee permanent neutrality as an assurance to Britain's security.

'Upon recognising Ireland's independence,' de Valera continued, 'England could at the same time issue a warning such as the Monroe Doctrine, that she would regard any attempt of any foreign power to obtain a foothold in Ireland as an act of hostility against herself. In case of a common foe Ireland's manpower would then be available for the defence of the two islands.'[15]

The President was following a carefully conceived policy. Privately he wrote that the 'best line to pursue' for propaganda purposes was to declare that Britain should 'propose a treaty with Ireland regarded as a separate state. Irish representatives would then be willing to consider making certain concessions to England's fear and England's interests.'[16] By thus appearing moderate he was keeping pressure on the British to negotiate. He was definitely opposed to standing openly for a republic and nothing short of it.

'There is no use in saying that DÁIL ÉIREANN cannot negotiate on account of the mandate which is given it,' de Valera explained to Harry Boland, 'that simply means that Lloyd George will be put in a position of being able to force an Irish Party into existence to oppose us at the next elections on the platform of "freedom to negotiate".'[17]

By emphasising the right of the Irish people to self-determination, however, the President could appear moderate without actually abandoning any republican aspirations. Thus it was possible to minimise the danger that some Irish party would be able to wean support away from Sinn Féin by portraying itself as a moderate peace party. 'In public statements,' de Valera advocated, 'our policy should be not to make it easy for Lloyd George by proclaiming that nothing but so and so will satisfy us. Our position should be simply that we are insisting on only one right, and that is the right of the people of this country to determine for themselves how they should be governed. That sounds moderate, but includes everything and puts Lloyd George, the Labour Party and others on the defensive, and apologetic as far as the world is concerned.'[18]

Seán T. O'Kelly, the Irish representative in Paris, was critical of the President's moderate approach. He thought the Dáil should adopt the line that the republican position was not negotiable, which annoyed de Valera, who felt that O'Kelly should concentrate on the French mission and not dabble in policy matters by making hardline statements. 'I wish he would confine himself to his own country,' the President wrote, 'and I am sending him a message to that effect.'[19]

As O'Kelly's wife, Cáit, was due to visit Paris, the President asked her to explain the advantages of advocating a settlement on the lines of the Cuban parallel suggested in the *Westminster Gazette* interview the previous year. De Valera explained his views to her, and she passed them on to her husband, but the latter was not impressed. 'I have not the least wish or intention to make myself troublesome,' O'Kelly wrote to the President on 17 April 1921, 'but lest you should have to say later, why did not people protest in time, I hold seriously — and I shall be astonished if some others will not be found who think as I — I hold that the firm stand we take "on an Irish Republic or nothing" needs not *change* but *development*.'[20]

De Valera was so attached to his own proposal he could not understand how anyone could disagree with it. He felt O'Kelly must have misunderstood it. The President therefore rebuked Cáit O'Kelly for probably having misrepresented the Cuban analogy in her conversation with her husband. If it were not for the possibility of such misrepresentation, de Valera wrote, 'I would have regarded his letter as incomprehensible and even worse. Considerable friction and very serious misunderstanding might have resulted. I can never allow such risks to be run again.'[21]

That same day the President sent a stern letter to O'Kelly

himself. 'Our representatives abroad,' he wrote, 'whether they be members of the Dáil or not, must regard themselves unequivocally the direct agents of the Department of Foreign Affairs, and must carry out the instructions of the Department, whether they personally agree with the policy or not.' Although representatives could legitimately raise objections in their correspondence with the Department of Foreign Affairs, he stressed that where the department insisted on a stand, 'it is only by resignation that the representatives can find a way out.'[22]

Shortly afterwards de Valera did receive a resignation, which he did not accept with grace. He had offered the post of ambassador to the United States to James O'Mara, but the latter, who was already furious that his advice on American matters was being repeatedly ignored by the President, had no intention of accepting the offer. O'Mara wrote privately that he could not 'continue to hold any official position under the government of the Irish Republic whose President claims such arbitrary executive authority, and in whose judgment of American affairs I have no longer any confidence.'[23] He not only refused to take the post offered to him but also sent de Valera his resignation as one of the three trustees of Dáil Éireann, in addition to announcing his decision not to stand for re-election to the Dáil the following month.

As O'Mara had gone to the United States to organise the Bond-certificate Drive and only stayed on at the beseeching of the President, he was entitled to expect that his resignation would be politely — if not graciously — accepted, but de Valera was in no mood to do either. Piqued at the resignation, he responded rather high-handedly with a telegram announcing that O'Mara was being fired — ignoring the fact that he had already submitted his resignation.[24]

In retrospect, however, the President's difficulties with O'Kelly and O'Mara were minor when compared with the eventual impact of his growing estrangement from Collins, who could be very brash and outspoken. The latter had previously antagonised many colleagues — especially Brugha and Stack — with his caustic comments and interference in their affairs, and the President soon became similarly irritated. It is not possible to be precise as to when the difficulties between them actually began to arise, but de Valera did tell his authorised biographers that from April 1921 onwards 'Collins did not seem to accept my view of things as he had done before and was inclined to give public expression to his own opinions even when they differed from mine.'[25] During April while de Valera was trying to portray a moderate image, Collins took a most uncompromising line in an interview with a celebrated American journalist, Carl Ackerman.[26]

Unlike de Valera, who tended to adopt a harder line in private than in public, Collins seemed to do the opposite and take firmer stands publicly. Collins was, in fact, considerably more moderate than the public image he projected. The British, believing that the President was looking for a negotiated settlement while Collins wanted a military solution, actually concluded that there was a power struggle within Sinn Féin in which Collins was the real leader and de Valera little more than a figure head.[27]

On 12 May 1921 when Winston Churchill, then British Minister for War, urged his government to seek a negotiated settlement because its existing policy was giving Britain an 'odious reputation' and was poisoning the country's relations with the United States, most of his colleagues were opposed to the idea, because they believed it would be wrong to deal with Collins and pointless talking with de Valera.[28]

The British had to reassess the situation a fortnight later after a large force of the IRA attacked the Customs House in Dublin and inflicted in the process the heaviest casualties since the Easter Rebellion of 1916. The IRA was seriously weakened by its own losses in the encounter, but the publicity generated had the effect of forcing the British to change their policy, which was essentially what de Valera had hoped for when he first advocated major military engagements.

They decided initially to intensify their campaign in Ireland, but before implementing the policy they temporised for fear of arousing public opinion. At that point Jan Christian Smuts, the South African Prime Minister who was in London for an Imperial Conference, persuaded Lloyd George that the time was ripe for negotiations. Since the Six Counties had been given Home Rule he argued that Britain would no longer have to contend with the Ulster question which had hampered a settlement in the past. Lloyd George then reversed his policy and invited de Valera and whomever he wished to accompany him as representatives of the majority in the Twenty-six Counties to meet with himself and Sir James Craig, the new Prime Minister of Northern Ireland, in a conference to try to settle the Irish question.

During the subsequent negotiations, which eventually led to the signing of the Anglo-Irish Treaty, de Valera initially played the dominant Irish role before withdrawing into the background. The negotiations can be divided into two distinct phases. The first consisted of preliminary sparring involving de Valera in a meeting with Smuts, three meetings with Unionist representatives from the Twenty-six Counties, and four private meetings with Lloyd George in London. Afterwards the President exchanged some letters with Smuts before entering a protracted correspondence with Lloyd George on procedural matters relating to setting up a conference in London. The second phase of the negotiations, throughout which de Valera remained in the background, revolved around the actual conference which convened on 11 October 1921 and concluded eight weeks later with the signing of the Anglo-Irish Treaty.

On meeting Smuts on 5 July 1921 de Valera revealed that he planned to reject Lloyd George's initial invitation on the grounds that it was a trap as participating in a conference in which a representative from the Six Counties would be on equal terms would provide tacit recognition of partition. Moreover, the President was afraid if Craig were included, the British would exploit the inevitable differences that would develop between the Irish factions and blame the failure of the conference on the inability of the Irish to agree among themselves. Consequently de Valera, who was demanding a truce before formal talks could begin, explained that he would not participate in the proposed tripartite conference.

Anxious to be able to give the British some idea of the kind of peace terms the Irish would be looking for, Smuts questioned the President. 'What do you propose as a solution of the Irish question?' he asked.[29]

'A republic,' replied de Valera.

'Do you really think that the British people are ever likely to agree to such a republic?'

The President explained that the attainment of republican status was so desirable that Irish representatives would agree to be bound by treaty limitations guaranteeing Britain's legitimate security needs, but he emphasised they would not be prepared to accept any restrictions under dominion status. In short, he insisted, according to Smuts, that the 'Irish people should have [the] choice between [a] republic plus treaty limitations and Dominion status without limitations.'[30]

'We want a free choice,' de Valera emphasised. 'Not a choice where the alternative is force. We must not be bullied into a decision.'[31]

'The British people will never give you this choice,' Smuts replied. 'You are next door to them.' He then talked about the difficulties experienced by the Transvaal Republic during its short but troubled existence. He mentioned that when the South African people were subsequently asked if they wanted a republic, 'a very large majority' preferred 'free partnership' within the British Empire. 'As a friend, I cannot advise you too strongly against a republic,' he added. 'Ask what you want but not a republic.'[32]

'If the status of Dominion rule is offered,' de Valera said, 'I will use all our machinery to get the Irish people to accept it.'[33]

Next day Smuts reported on his Irish visit to a cabinet level meeting in London, where it was decided to accede to de Valera's demands for both a truce and the exclusion of Craig from the conference. Lloyd George, however, left it to Smuts to get de Valera to take the initiative for Craig's exclusion.

The South African leader wrote to de Valera that there was no reason why Dublin should not demand the conference be restricted to the two major contending parties, but he advised that the Ulster question should be played down. 'I see no objection to your stating that the dispute is now between the Irish majority and the British Government, and the conference for a settlement should be between the two,' he wrote. 'But the less said about Ulster the better, for fear of giving unnecessary umbrage in that quarter or making things more difficult for yourself hereafter.'[34]

The President kept that advice in mind when he wrote to Lloyd George on 8 July 1921. Carefully sidestepping the whole question of a tripartite conference, he simply agreed to meet the British leader so that they could discuss 'on what basis such a conference as that proposed can reasonably hope to achieve peace.'

Although four cabinet colleagues accompanied de Valera to London, he suggested, or rather intimated, that Lloyd George and himself should meet privately. 'For my own part,' the President wrote, 'I am quite ready, if you prefer it, to meet you alone.'[35] In the traditional accounts of their first meeting de Valera had been depicted as lecturing Lloyd George on British misrule in Ireland and only reaching the time of Cromwell by the end of the session, but the Prime Minister's own account of the proceedings provided a somewhat different picture. He noted that de Valera 'listened well' and had an agreeable personality.[36]

The Irish leader actually planned to show as little of his own hand as possible. He wanted the British to make an offer so that the Dáil would then 'be free to consider it without prejudice.'[37] Hence he was prepared to allow Lloyd George to do most of the talking.

The tactics proved successful. Unable to pin down de Valera, the Prime Minister became so frustrated during the first three meetings, which he compared to being on a merry-go-round one horse behind the President and totally unable to catch up, that he put forward specific proposals on 20 July 1921. These offered the Twenty-six Counties a form of dominion status which was curtailed by an insistence on free trade and by defence stipulations restricting the size of the Irish army, prohibiting a navy, and insisting upon guarantees that Britain could obtain whatever naval and air facilities she might desire in time of war. The proposals also stipulated that the new Irish state should 'allow for full recognition of the existing powers and privileges of the parliament of Northern Ireland, which cannot be abrogated except by their own consent.'

De Valera later explained that he had anticipated such proposals would be made and realised that unless there was some acceptable alternative other than 'that of continuing the war for maintenance of the Republic, I felt certain that the majority of the people would be weaned from us.'[38] Consequently he was already thinking of a compromise formula to ensure that Ireland would have the freedom of unfettered dominion status. He was looking for the same *de facto* status of dominions like Canada and South Africa.

The crux of the problem was that dominion status itself would not guarantee Ireland the actual status of the dominions. They were free because they were so far from Britain that it was virtually impossible for Westminster to exercise its legal right to interfere in their internal affairs. Ireland, on the other hand, was so near Britain that Westminster could intervene in Irish affairs with impunity. In order to resolve this problem de Valera came up with External Association, although he had not given a name to his formula when he met with Lloyd George for the last time on 21 July 1921.

The President flatly rejected the British offer. Although he promised a considered reply after he had a chance to consult with his colleagues in Dublin, he proceeded to give an idea of what he had in mind. He intimated, according to Lloyd George, that he would be willing to accept 'the status of a dominion *sans phrase* on condition that Northern Ireland would agree to be represented within an all-Ireland parliament, otherwise de Valera insisted that the only alternative was for the Twenty-six Counties to be a republic.'[39]

As the British document was really a significant advance on anything previously offered to Ireland, de Valera had to be careful that his formal rejection would not afford the Westminster government the opportunity of enlisting the public support deemed necessary for an all-out campaign to suppress the Sinn Féin movement. If he took too hard a line with the British, it could be particularly damaging in the vital propaganda struggle, but a weak stand would undermine the Irish position for the subsequent negotiations. The President therefore adopted the somewhat circuitous tactic of communicating with Smuts, knowing that the latter was keeping in close touch with the British. Thus, by taking a hard line in his correspondence with the South African leader, de Valera effectively gave the British an uncompromising reply without actually exposing himself to the pitfalls of such response sent directly to Lloyd George.

'I was greatly disappointed with the British Government's proposals', de Valera wrote to Smuts on 21 July 1921. 'They seem quite unable to understand the temper of our people, or appear not to have the will to realise the opportunity that is now presented to them.' He added that much further 'suffering would seem to be in store for our people.'

Smuts, who was actually one of the authors of the British document, responded with a reasoned appeal supporting it. Knowing that Sinn Féin feared that Ireland's proximity to Britain would prevent her from enjoying the real freedom of the dominions, the South African leader argued that dominion status would really strengthen Irish independence. As a dominion Ireland could readily expect help from the other dominions if Britain tried to interfere in Irish affairs, because if such interference went unchallenged it would be tantamount to admitting that Britain had a right to interfere in the affairs of all the dominions. He went on to argue that the attainment of dominion status in the Twenty-six Counties also offered an opportunity of breaking down the distrust that had led to partition. 'Start as a full Dominion,' Smuts wrote, 'make a succcess of self-government in the South, and it will not be long before the North will agree to join hands with you freely and willingly.'[40]

In reply the following week, de Valera explained that the partition issue was of paramount importance. 'Unless the North East comes in on some reasonable basis,' he wrote, 'no further progress can be made.' If that obstacle could be overcome, he held out the possibility of accommodation on other matters, as Ireland was anxious to be on friendly terms with Britain and the dominions. Nevertheless he stressed that it was 'only in freedom that friendship could come.' As the Irish people were 'devotedly attached' to the principle of national self-determination, of which 'the Republic is the expression', he warned that they would not readily abandon their position on the issue, but would be 'prepared to make great sacrifices in other directions.'[41]

Continuing in terms that were to have ominous implications for the future, the President declared 'the questions of procedure and form as distinguished from substance are very important.' When he told both Smuts and Lloyd George that he was prepared to accept the 'status of a dominion', he apparently did not mean that he was willing to agree to dominion status. This was where the distinction between form and substance was important. In substance, dominion status and the status of a dominion were the same, but the form envisioned by de Valera for the latter was different. When he spoke of the 'status of a dominion', he envisioned Ireland as an independent nation *outside* the British Commonwealth but ready to accept the real obligations of the countries within the Commonwealth. It was in the manner in which Ireland accepted those obligations that procedure was important. He wanted a procedure followed whereby Britain would, in effect, at first acknowledge Irish freedom, and Ireland would then freely accept the same *de facto* status as the dominions but without actually going back into the British Commonwealth. As the British did not seem to appreciate the merits of such an approach, he hoped that Smuts would prolong his stay in Britain and try to win them over.

Smuts did seriously consider delaying his return home. He sent his secretary to Dublin and Belfast in order to explore the possibility of playing a further role in the negotiations, but it quickly became apparent that there were going to be serious difficulties concerning partition, because de Valera was insisting on the ending of partition before he would compromise on the question of association with the British Empire, and Craig was unwilling to consider Irish unity outside the United Kingdom. Consequently the South African leader concluded that there was an *impasse*.

'Both you and Craig are equally immovable,' he wrote to de Valera. 'Force as a solution of the problem is out of the question, both on your side and his premises. The process of arriving at an agreement will therefore take time.'[42]

Following the South African Premier's departure de Valera wrote to Lloyd George on 10 August 1921 formally rejecting the British proposals. In the letter, which was essentially a restatement of earlier arguments, the President explained that the restrictive conditions of the July proposals, which were unheard of in the case of the dominions, would be an interference in Irish affairs. Nevertheless he reiterated his willingness to compromise in return for an assurance of Irish unity:

> A certain treaty of free association with the British Commonwealth group, as with a partial league of nations, we would be ready to recommend, and as a Government to negotiate and take responsibility for, had we an assurance that the entry of the nation as a whole in such an association would secure it the allegiance of the present dissenting minority, to meet whose sentiments alone this step could be contemplated.

He added that if the British would stand aside, the Irish factions would settle partition between themselves without resorting to arms. 'We agree with you,' he wrote, '"that no common action can be secured by force".'

Back in 1918 de Valera had concluded that the British had undermined the Irish Convention by assuring Ulster Unionists that they could not be coerced. Bolstered by that assurance the Unionists insisted on having their own way, with the result that when the nationalists balked, the Convention inevitably ended in failure. 'It was evident to us,' de Valera wrote shortly afterwards, that 'with the "coercion-of-Ulster is unthinkable" guarantee, the Unionists would solidly maintain their original position.'[43] Consequently when de Valera gave the British a similar assurance himself, he was obviously thinking that partition might have to be accepted as part of an overall settlement. Indeed he told a private session of the Dáil on 22 August 1921 that, if Britain would recognise the Irish Republic, then he 'would be in favour of giving each county power to vote itself out of the Republic if it so wished.'[44] The only choice would be to coerce Northern Ireland, which was a policy for which he would not accept responsibility. He did not think that coercion would be successful, and he warned his colleagues that if they tried to use force against the North, they would be making the same mistake with the majority there that the British had made with the rest of the island.

De Valera actually admitted to the Dáil that he was not excluding the possibility of any kind of settlement with Britain. Before allowing his name to go forward for re-election as President, he declared he would not be bound to any particular form of government by his republican oath. 'Remember I do not take, as far as I am concerned, oaths as regards forms of Government,' he declared. 'I regard myself here to maintain the independence of Ireland and to do the best for the Irish people.' He would, he insisted, feel free to consider any proposals that were consistent with 'what I consider the people of Ireland want and what I consider is best from their point of view.'[45]

'I cannot accept office,' he added, 'except on the understanding that no road is barred, [and] that we shall be free to consider every method.' The policy of the cabinet, he explained would be to do what he thought best for the country and 'those who would disagree with me would resign.'

De Valera was duly re-elected President, and he appointed a seven man cabinet consisting of himself, Griffith, Collins, Austin Stack, Cathal Brugha, Robert Barton, and W. T. Cosgrave. One of the more significant features of his appointments was the allocation of the portfolio of Foreign Affairs to Griffith. Prior to the truce the President had indicated that he intended to retain the post, which he had earlier described as 'the one for which I feel the most immediate personal responsibility.'[46] Although he had designated George Nobel Count Plunkett as Minister for Foreign Affairs in his first government, the President nevertheless effectively took over the post himself upon returning from the United States. He did instruct the secretary of the department to consult with Plunkett, but explained that there was no need for personal interviews with the minister. 'Just keep him fairly well informed,' de Valera wrote, 'and do him the courtesy of asking his opinion now and then on important matters.'[47]

The significance of Griffith's appointment soon became apparent when de Valera told his new cabinet that he did not plan to take part in the forthcoming negotiations with the British. He explained that whoever went to Britain would have to compromise and by staying at home he would be able to rally the Irish people to fight for an absolute claim, rather than a compromise, in the event that the fight had to be restarted.[48] He wrote many years later, 'the views of the "moderates", some Church leaders and others, those who would have been willing to accept a form of "home rule", had in this case of a "break" obviously to be kept in mind.' Since the rejection of the July proposals Lloyd George had been deliberately trying to create the impression that the Irish leader was 'an impossible person, one with whom no one could do business,' and de Valera found that some of the moderates at home were now propagating this as a fact. 'To meet their case it was better that the "break" should not come directly through me, but rather through one whom they regarded as more "moderate",' he wrote. 'Were there to be a "break" with any substantial section of our people discontented and restless, the national position would be dangerously weakened when the war resumed. I was providing for this contingency much better by remaining at home than by leading the delegation.'[49]

On the other hand, if an agreement were reached on the lines of External Association, which was a plan that had been evolving in de Valera's mind ever since he first suggested an Irish settlement on the lines of the independence accorded to Cuba around the turn of the century, he knew there would be 'sharp differences' at home, and he contended that he would be in a much better position to influence radical republicans to accept a compromise agreement, if he were not a party to the negotiations himself.[50] 'It was almost certain,' he later explained, 'that it would be no easy task to get that settlement accepted whole-heartedly by the Dáil and by the Army. The arrangement was a novel one. The kind of association involved was new to our public opinion.' He added that the whole idea was likely to be resisted by some of the more radical separatists, with the result that there would have to be 'a critical campaign' to convince them. 'My influence in that campaign,' he wrote, 'would be vastly more effective if I myself were not a member of the negotiating team, and so completely free from any suggestion that I had been affected by the "London atmosphere".'[51] In emphasising that point at the cabinet meeting an allusion was made to the difficulties that had bedevilled Woodrow Wilson when he tried to secure American ratification of the Versailles Treaty having been personally involved in the Paris peace talks.[52]

Some members of the cabinet were unconvinced by the President's arguments. They insisted he should attend the conference, and a vote was taken. Griffith, Collins and Cosgrave called for his inclusion, but Brugha, Stack and Barton supported him. He was able to use his own casting vote to exclude himself. He then proposed that Griffith should lead the delegation and be accompanied by Stack, Brugha and Collins. Griffith was amenable, but the others refused. Brugha and Stack were absolutely adamant, while Collins contended he could be of more use to the delegation by staying at home. In essence he put forward similar arguments for his own exclusion as those put forward by the President.

'I was somewhat surprised at his reluctance,' de Valera wrote, 'for he had been rather annoyed with me for not bringing him on the team when I went to meet Lloyd George earlier on in July. I now considered it essential that he should be on the team with Griffith.'[53] Griffith and Collins were logical choices as both had personal followings of their own within the movement. Griffith had a great influence on the older members of Sinn Féin, while the IRB and the younger gunmen tended to look to Collins. The President's chances of getting a compromise settlement accepted in Dublin would be considerably enhanced if both of them were involved in the settlement.

'It is not a question of individuals now,' de Valera said to Collins. 'It is a question of the nation and you and I and the Cabinet know that the British will not make their best offer in your absence.'[54]

In spite of strong personal misgivings Collins, who feared that de Valera was setting him up as a scapegoat, reluctantly agreed to go to London out of a sense of duty.[55] Three others were then chosen to work in well with himself and Griffith. Of those only Robert Barton was a member of the cabinet. The other two, George Gavan Duffy and Eamon Duggan, were lawyers who were included, according to de Valera, as 'mere legal padding'.[56]

When the Dáil was asked to confirm the selection of the delegates with plenipotentiary powers, there was some talk of limiting their authority, but de Valera was adamantly opposed. In fact, he had already threatened to resign as President if the delegation was not given full plenipotentiary authority, and he had his way.[57] The cabinet did, nevertheless, issue secret instructions stipulating that the delegation should keep in touch with the ministers remaining in Dublin about the progress of the negotiations, should send a copy of any draft treaty about to be signed, and should await a reply from Dublin before signing it. Although these instructions were accepted by the delegation, they were not binding, as the Dáil had already conferred full plenipotentiary powers on the delegation. Consequently in any instance in which the instructions from the cabinet, an inferior body, infringed on the powers conferred by the Dáil, the instructions were void.

The instructions were issued so that de Valera could keep an eye on both Griffith and Collins, whom, he felt certain, were contemplating a more moderate settlement than he had in mind in that they would ulimately be prepared to agree to dominion status under the British Crown. 'That Griffith would accept the Crown under pressure I had no doubt,' the President wrote, adding that from reports of the work that Collins was doing within the IRB 'and from my own weighing up of him, I felt certain that he too was contemplating accepting the Crown, but I had hoped that all this would simply make them both a better bait for Lloyd George — leading him on and on, further in our direction.' De Valera was confident of being able to prevent members of the delegation from conceding too much. 'I felt convinced,' he wrote, 'that as matters came to a close we would be able to hold them from this side from crossing the line.'[58]

His confidence was based on essentially three factors. One, the delegation would be reporting on the progress of the negotiations. Two, he thought Barton 'would be strong and stubborn enough as a retarding force to any precipitate giving away by the delegation.' And three, Erskine Childers, who shared the President's ideological outlook, had been appointed chief secretary to the delegation, so he would be able to keep an eye on the plenipotentiaries and 'would give Barton, his relative and close friend, added strength.' The two of them were not only double first cousins but Childers had been reared by Barton's parents, with the result that Barton himself was like a younger brother. 'I felt,' de Valera wrote, 'that with these in touch with the delegation, and the cabinet at home hanging on to their coat-tails everything was safe for the tug-of-war.'[59]

Before the conference could begin, however, there was a diplomatic stumbling block to be cleared. In accepting Lloyd George's initial invitation to send a delegation to Britain, de Valera had asserted that the Irish team would be representing a nation which recognised itself as independent. He later clarified this by explaining that he did not expect the British to recognise Irish independence but was merely stating the fact that the Irish representatives recognised their country as such. But Lloyd George was unwilling to have any confusion on that point. Not only would Britain not recognise Irish independence, but he stressed that there could be no talks if Irish representatives persisted with their own self-recognition. The Prime Minister again emphasised this in his telegram of 29 September 1921 in which he renewed the invitation to the conference.

In reply, next day, de Valera accepted the invitation.

'Our respective positions have been stated and are understood,' he declared. The President was apparently trying to give the impression that he was still insisting on self-recognition, but of course he had simply made a statement, not set a condition. He, in effect, acknowledged that there could be no conference if the Irish side persisted in claiming self-recognition. This was to have a profound significance shortly after the conference began.

When the Irish plenipotentiaries went to London they were supposed to try to secure a settlement on the lines of External Association, but they only had what Barton described as 'a hazy conception' of what it would be in its final form. What was clear to them was that no vestige of British authority should remain in the internal affairs of Ireland, although the country would agree to association with the British Commonwealth on external or international matters.[60]

The plenipotentiaries were furnished with a partially completed document known as Draft Treaty A, in which External Association was outlined in treaty form. It stipulated Ireland should be recognised 'as a sovereign independent state' and Britain should renounce 'all claims to govern or to legislate' for the island. In return, Ireland would then become externally associated with the British Commonwealth, enjoying equal status with the dominions and being separately represented at Imperial Conferences. Instead of the common citizenship of those in the dominions, however, External Association envisaged reciprocal citizenship — the subtle difference being that the Irish people would be Irish citizens rather than British subjects, but they would nevertheless enjoy the same rights and privileges as British subjects while residing within the British Commonwealth, and British subjects would enjoy reciprocal rights with Irish citizens while resident in Ireland. It was thought necessary to seek reciprocal rights because de Valera was afraid that Irish people throughout the British Empire would withdraw their sympathy if the Dáil sought a settlement that would make them aliens. In some respects the distinction between reciprocal and common citizenship represented on an individual level the difference between External Association and dominion status at the national level.[61]

De Valera's controversial suggestion regarding the first article of the Platt Amendment was the inspiration for a further aspect of Draft Treaty A which called for the British Commonwealth to guarantee 'the perpetual neutrality of Ireland and the integrity and inviolability of Irish territory.' In return Ireland would commit 'itself to enter into no compact, and take no action, nor permit any action to be taken, inconsistent with the obligation of preserving its own neutrality and inviolability and to repel with force any attempt to violate its territory or to use its territorial waters for warlike purposes.' Once ratified by the respective parliaments or by the people, if submitted to them by either the Dáil or Westminster, the Treaty would be registered at Geneva, where the member states of the British Commonwealth would undertake to try to get 'the formal recognition of Ireland's neutrality, integrity and inviolability by the League of Nations in conformity with the similar guaranteees in favour of Switzerland.' Britain would also try to secure formal recognition of that perpetual neutrality by those states that were not members of the League with whom she had diplomatic relations, such as the United States, Germany and the Soviet Union.

Notwithstanding its appearance, Draft Treaty A was not really supposed to be the outline for a contemplated treaty, as has sometimes been supposed. Instead it contained counter-proposals that the Irish delegation would put forward for negotiating purposes in response to Britain's proposals of 20 July. De Valera actually proposed that the Irish side should draw up a series of contingency draft treaties. Draft Treaty B, for instance, would be the document that the plenipotentiaries would publish as terms acceptable to them in the event of the London conference collapsing. The President gave Duffy and Childers incomplete copies of these two draft treaties on the eve of their departure, but he did not attempt to draft the document that they were supposed to use for a contemplated treaty. They would have to be responsible for that drafting. 'We must depend on your side for the initiative after this,' the

President wrote to Griffith.[62] In the light of subsequent events, the use of the words 'your side' was certainly ominous.

The conference was only into its second week when de Valera caused considerable uneasiness in his relations with the leadership of the delegation by reviving the self-recognition issue without telling those in London. In fact, it was only on reading the morning newspapers they learned that a controversy had been caused by the publication of an open telegram the President had sent to Pope Benedict XV in response to an exchange of telegrams between the Pope and King George V. In his telegram de Valera complained that in expressing the hope that the negotiations would 'achieve a permanent settlement of the troubles in Ireland and may initiate a new era of peace and happiness for my people' the British King had implied the Irish strife was an internal British problem and that the Irish people owed allegiance to the King whereas, he contended, Ireland had already declared her independence. De Valera was actually using the King's message, which was vague enough to be interpreted differently, to take an indirect slap at the Pope, whose telegram was the really irritating one from the Irish standpoint because in addressing the King, de Valera explained, 'the Vatican recognised the struggle between Ireland and England as a purely domestic one, for King George, and by implication pronounced judgment against us.'[63]

Under the circumstances it was understandable that Griffith and Collins were annoyed that while they were involved in delicate negotiations the President had revived the recognition controversy by insulting the British King in an attempt to chide the Pope. Moreover, Collins, who was already deeply suspicious, feared that de Valera was preparing the ground to blame the delegation for any compromise by covering up the fact that the claim of self-recognition had been shelved when the invitation to the conference was accepted. Another particularly irritating feature of the whole affair was that it brought the question of the Crown, which the Irish delegation had hoped to leave until last, to the forefront of the negotiations.

Initially no role was envisaged for the Crown in line with External Association. De Valera actually warned the delegation on 25 October 1921 that members of the cabinet in Dublin were unanimously of the opinion there could be no question 'of our asking the Irish people to enter an arrangement which would make them subject to the Crown, or demand from them allegiance to the British King. If war is the alternative we can only face it, and I think that the sooner the other side is made to recognise that the better.'[64] External Association evolved somewhat in the following days, and the cabinet agreed to recognise the British King as the head of the proposed External Association to which Ireland would belong.

During the conference the Irish delegation followed basically the same approach as had been pursued by de Valera. In return for a guarantee of Irish unity the plenipotentiaries offered to agree to External Association, which was depicted simply as a means of ensuring that Ireland would have the real constitutional status enjoyed by the dominions, rather than the technical legal position. The problem was that legally the British Crown had the right to veto all British and dominion legislation, with the result that the King was an absolute monarch in theory. Under the unwritten British constitutional system, however, those powers had been eroded with the result that the Crown no longer enjoyed that veto power. Moreover, if the British parliament wished to instruct the King to make use of his legal powers in the case of the dominions, they were too far away from Britain, which would not be able to use her *de jure* right to interfere in their internal affairs. Ireland, on the other hand, was so close that Britain could act in the name of the Crown to interfere in Irish affairs at will. The Irish representatives therefore argued that while the British King could be recognised as head of an External Association, it was essential that the Crown should be eliminated from internal Irish affairs. Ireland's independence would thus be protected from British intrigue, while Britain's legitimate needs would at the same time be assured. In essence, the Irish were contending that they were only trying to ensure that their country would have the *de facto* status of a dominion. Lloyd George undermined that argument by offering to include in a treaty any phrase that the Irish wanted to 'ensure that the position of the Crown in Ireland should be no more in practice than it was in Canada or in any other dominion.' Griffith felt that the Irish case for External Association had been destroyed. 'With this offer,' he wrote, 'they knocked out my argument.'[65] He might just as well have written that they had undermined de Valera's own line of argument because the President had been pursuing that line himself.

In order to fulfil their instructions the plenipotentiaries returned to Dublin on 3 December 1921 to discuss with the cabinet members there what were supposed to be the final British terms. Subject to certain specified exceptions — mainly on defensive matters — the British offered the Irish Free State, as Ireland would be known, the same status as the dominions in 'law, practice and constitutional usage'. The exceptions, which really limited Irish freedom in comparison with the dominions, were in matters of trade and defence. The British insisted on free trade, while the defence clauses stipulated that the coastal defence of Britain and Ireland would 'be undertaken exclusively' by the British, who would retain control of four specified Irish ports and any other facilities that might be desired 'in times of war or of strained relations with a foreign Power.' In addition, the size of the Free State's army would be in proportion to the Irish population as the British army was to the population of Britain. Another specific difference was the form of the oath to be taken by members of the Irish parliament.

The Irish had objected to the oath being used in Canada. Instead of swearing direct allegiance to the King, they suggested an oath to the Irish constitution. The British came up with the compromise proposal that members of the Free State parliament should swear 'allegiance to the Constitution of the Irish Free State; to the Community of Nations known as the British Empire; and to the King as Head of the State and of the Empire.'

On the Ulster question the draft treaty gave a fleeting recognition to Irish unity in that it would apply to the whole island although Northern Ireland representatives were not consulted, but it did protect Unionist interests by stipulating that Northern Ireland could decide to retain her existing status. In that event, however, a Boundary Commission would be established to re-adjust the boundary of Northern Ireland 'in accordance with the wishes of the inhabitants, so far as may be compatible with economic and geographic conditions.'

At the outset of the cabinet meeting each of the plenipotentiaries gave his views on the draft treaty. Griffith explained that he was in favour of the proposals, and Duggan supported him. Collins, too, was 'in substantial agreement', but he did suggest that the oath should not be accepted.[66] Both Barton and Duffy believed that further concessions could be wrung from the British, so they advocated rejecting the proposals.

De Valera objected to the draft treaty on the grounds that the oath was unacceptable, and he criticised the clauses allowing Northern Irealnd to vote itself out of the Irish state. He said that he could understand accepting dominion status in return for national unity, but the proposals afforded neither one nor the other. He also took exception to the stipulation that the British would have the exclusive right of defending Irish coastal waters, although he did think 'it natural for them to demand facilities on our coast as being necessary.' He said that he would be prepared to give them *'only two bases'* instead of the four being demanded.[67] He concluded by suggesting that the delegates should go back to London, try to have the document amended, and, if necessary, face the consequence of war.

Arguing that it was unfair to ask Griffith to break on the Crown when he was unwilling to fight on the issue, Barton proposed that de Valera himself should return to London with them. The President was seriously considering the suggestion, when Griffith emphasised his own attitude. After as many concessions as possible had been gained, the Chairman of the delegation said that he would sign the treaty and go before the Dáil, which was the body to decide for or against war.

'Don't you realise that, if you sign this thing, you will

split Ireland from top to bottom?' Brugha interjected.

'I suppose that's so,' replied Griffith, apparently struck by the implication of Brugha's words. 'I'll tell you what I'll do. I'll go back to London. I'll not sign the document, but I'll bring it back and submit it to the Dáil and, if necessary to the people.'[68]

Satisfied with the assurance, de Valera decided there was no need for himself to join the delegation. When the plenipotentiaries asked for suggestions on an alternative oath, the President proposed two or three different forms, but he made little other effort to suggest counter-proposals. One of the truly extraordinary features of the meeting was the fact that Collins left believing that the offer of *de facto* dominion status was acceptable to the President. Even Childers, who was deeply attached to the concept of External Association, was unsure what de Valera wanted, so just before the meeting ended he asked if in proposing a new oath the President also wished the delegation to stand by the demand for External Association.[69]

'Yes,' replied de Valera, and Childers was satisfied.[70] Collins, possibly pre-occupied with preparations to leave, never heard the exchange. He had thought that the cabinet was satisfied with the guarantee of the *de facto* status of Canada. In the light of subsequent events, it was astonishing that the President should have treated the association question so lightly at the cabinet meeting, because the issue was soon to become a fundamental basis for his opposition to the Treaty signed in London early on the morning of 6 December 1921.

CHAPTER FOUR

# No Right To Do Wrong

*Events Leading to the Civil War*

De Valera was in Limerick on 6 December 1921 when he learned that an agreement had been signed in London. 'I never thought they would give in so soon!' he exclaimed on being told the news.[1] In view of Griffith's undertaking not to sign the draft treaty, the President somehow concluded that the British must have conceded External Association. He was therefore delighted. 'I felt like throwing my hat in the air,' he wrote.[2]

After the terms of the Treaty were published, however, he issued a statement to the effect that the cabinet members in London had 'to report at once so that a full cabinet decision may be taken.'[3] There followed a somewhat stormy cabinet meeting on 8 December. The plenipotentiaries related the circumstances leading to their signing. Barton explained that he had agreed to sign only after Lloyd George had threatened him with immediate and terrible war if he refused to do so. But Griffith refused to admit that there had been any coercion as far as he was concerned, which was correct, as he had agreed to sign before Lloyd George issued the ultimatum.

Having warned Smuts some months earlier that Ireland would have to have a free choice and not be forced to accept any settlement, it was hardly surprising that de Valera came out against the Treaty. Yet he seemed even more annoyed that the plenipotentiaries had accepted terms other than External Association without first consulting him. They were, he charged, guilty 'of an act of disloyalty to their President and to their colleagues in the Cabinet such as is probably without parallel in history.'[4] Ironically none of the delegation had thought it necessary to consult those in Dublin, as the draft treaty had been discussed with them the previous weekend. Of course, Griffith had promised not to sign that document. Had it not been for that undertaking, the President said that he would have gone to London and rejected the British terms himself. 'I would,' he explained, 'have gone and said "Go to the devil, I will not sign".'[5]

Griffith denied that he had gone back on any undertaking, as the delegation had secured some very significant changes in the British terms before signing. There was a new oath (which had been proposed by Collins), and modifications in the defence clauses — including the removal of the stipulation granting Britain the exclusive right to defend the seas around Ireland. The draft terms were actually amended to allow the Free State to have her own naval vessels for fishery and revenue protection, and there was a stipulation to the effect that the whole defence question would be reconsidered in five years 'with a view to the undertaking by Ireland of a share in her own coastal defence.' The British had also abandoned their demand for free trade, so Griffith argued that he had not violated his undertaking not to sign the document discussed at the cabinet. Even de Valera admitted that the Treaty 'considerably differed' from the draft proposals presented to the cabinet.[6] In that case, however, the Treaty was a different document and should as a result have been submitted to the cabinet in accordance with the instructions. The President was therefore justified in thinking that Griffith either broke the verbal undertaking given at the cabinet meeting, or else violated the instructions, although none of the plenipotentiaries had realised that before the signing.

De Valera himself must share some of the blame for the misunderstanding. In fact, Barton accused him of being responsible for the mess because of his refusal to go to London. At some stage or another, for instance, all three cabinet members on the delegation had urged him to go to London. He had also refused to intervene when Duffy and Childers complained at different times about the way Griffith and Collins were conducting the negotiations. Yet he had saddled a delegation of moderates with the full responsibility to negotiate and conclude a settlement. 'The disaster was,' Barton said, '*we were not a fighting delegation.*'[7]

De Valera did not question the actual right of the plenipotentiaries to sign the Treaty. Indeed, his first reaction to the news that an agreement had been signed clearly demonstrated that he believed, notwithstanding the commitment to refer the Treaty to Dublin before signing, the delegates had a right to sign without referring it back. He later stressed that point repeatedly in the Dáil. 'Now I would like everybody clearly to understand,' he declared, 'that the plenipotentiaries went over to negotiate a Treaty, that they could differ from the cabinet if they wanted to, and that in anything of consequence they could take their decision against the decision of the cabinet.'[8]

The cabinet divided fairly evenly on the Treaty. Cosgrave joined Griffith and Collins in favour of the agreement, while the President, Brugha, and Stack lined up in opposition, so it was Barton's vote which made the difference. Although Barton was personally opposed to the Treaty, he supported it because he had committed himself to do so by signing the agreement in the first place.

De Valera was urged repeatedly to go along with the majority of the cabinet and not come out publicly against the Treaty, but he dismissed the appeals. He said that he had worked for a settlement which radicals like Brugha could accept. Indeed he had done a magnificent job of bringing Brugha, whom he described as 'a bit slow at seeing fine differences and rather stubborn,'[9] to the point where there was very little difference between him and what the British were offering. The President, however, charged that the chance of securing a united cabinet had been wrecked by the actions of the plenipotentiaries in signing the agreement without consulting those in Dublin. The cabinet was deeply split. De Valera declared that he would resign if the Treaty was accepted by the Dáil, while Griffith and Collins said that they would quit if it was rejected. In the interim, however, all agreed that they would stay on until the Dáil decided.[10]

Before the meeting concluded the President, who was still hopeful 'of winning better terms yet', announced that he was planning to put forward his own alternative proposals in the Dáil.[11] 'The greatest test of your people has come,' he declared in a statement prepared for the press that night. 'Let us face it worthily without bitterness, and above all, without recriminations. There is a definite constitutional way of resolving our political differences — let us not depart from it, and let the conduct of the cabinet in this matter be an example to the whole nation.' Next morning when he met Childers, he seemed 'certain of winning' with his alternative. Childers was amazed at his confidence.[12]

When the Dáil convened to consider the Treaty on 14 December 1921, the President persuaded the assembly to go into private session at which he could introduce his alternative. The transcript of that session, which lay unpublished for more than half a century, provides a valuable insight into his thinking on the whole controversy because he spoke repeatedly, often with amazing candor. He admitted, for instance, that there was only a small difference between the Treaty and what he would accept. In fact, he said that he did not believe that the British would go to war over 'that small difference' or for 'that little sentimental thing', as he referred to the extra concession on which he wanted to stand firm. 'I was ready to break if we didn't get it,' he said, 'because I felt that the distance between the two was so small that the British would not wage war on account of it. You say if it is so small why not take it. But I say, that small difference makes all the difference. This fight has lasted all through the centuries and I would be willing to win that little sentimental thing that would satisfy the aspirations of this country.'[13]

De Valera was so convinced of the validity of his own views that he believed others could be persuaded to hold out for 'that small difference'. The true test of his sincerity was his willingness to explain his position in detail. His alternative was drawn up in the form of a draft treaty, which became known as Document No. 2. Copies of it were given to every member of the Dáil in the hope of persuading them to substitute it for the Treaty.

Document No. 2 differed from the Treaty mainly in terms of association, the oath and defence. In accordance with the President's plan, for example, Ireland would be clearly an autochthonous state — that is, a state which derived its powers to govern from its own people rather than from some outside agency like the British parliament, as would be the case under the Treaty. This was important because if the British parliament had the acknowledged authority to grant powers of self-government to the Irish people, it would follow by implication that it could amend those same powers. The first clause of de Valera's alternative therefore stipulated that 'the legislative, executive, and judicial authority of Ireland shall be derived solely from the people of Ireland.'

Subsequent clauses specified, nevertheless, that Ireland would be associated with the British Commonwealth on matters of common concern in accordance with which she would enjoy 'the same privileges as the other dominions' with the respective citizens of Ireland and the dominions enjoying reciprocal rights. Matters of common concern were defined as:

> Defence, Peace and War, Political Treaties, and all matters now treated as of common concern amongst the States of the British Commonwealth, and that in these matters there shall be between Ireland and the States of the British Commonwealth 'such concerted action founded on consultation as the several Governments may determine.'

In other words Ireland would enjoy the same *de facto* freedom as the dominions and would assume the same responsibilities.

The defence clauses of Document No. 2 proposed giving Britain the same facilities as the Treaty but stipulated that after five years the British would hand 'over the coastal defence of Ireland to the Irish Government, unless some other arrangement for naval defence be agreed by both Governments.' This was a significant difference from the Treaty, which stipulated only that the two countries would reconsider the defence question after a similar period. Thus, de Valera was stipulating that if no other arrangement was made, then Ireland would assume complete control of her defence resources in five years.

The President's stand in regard to the Ulster question differed from the Treaty merely in that he wanted a stipulation added to the effect that in accepting the Treaty's partition clauses the Dáil would not be 'recognising the right of any part of Ireland to be excluded from the supreme authority of the National Parliament and Government.' Thus while Northern Ireland's right to secede would not be recognised, its actual secession would be accepted for the sake of 'internal peace, and in the desire to bring no force or coercion to bear upon any substantial part of the province of Ulster.' De Valera had suggested such a course because he was anxious to isolate the Ulster question from the overall Anglo-Irish dispute. 'The difficulty is not the Ulster question,' he explained. 'As far as we are concerned this is a fight between Ireland and England. I want to eliminate the Ulster question out of it.' Consequently, he was prepared to accept the partition clauses of the Treaty although he found them objectionable from the standpoint that they provided 'an explicit recognition of the right on the part of Irishmen to secede from Ireland.'[14] In short, he was prepared to accept Northern Ireland's secession but was anxious to create the impression that he was not formally acknowledging what he was in fact accepting. 'We will take the same things as agreed on there [in the Treaty],' he told the Dáil. 'Let us not start to fight with Ulster. Let us accept that, but put in a declaratory phrase which will safeguard our right.'[15]

A further difference between the Treaty and Document No. 2 was the omission of an oath from the latter. It merely stated that 'for the purposes of association, Ireland shall recognise his Britannic Majesty as head of the Association.' Nevertheless the President admitted during the private session that he had suggested at the cabinet meeting on 3 December that an oath would be acceptable. In fact, in an attempt to explain his position, he revealed that he had proposed the following oath:

> I, so and so, swear to obey the Constitution of Ireland and to keep faith with his Britannic Majesty, so and so, in respect of the treaty associating Ireland with the states of the British Commonwealth.

He went on to tell Dáil deputies that he would still 'be quite ready' to take that oath, if he was satisfied with the form of the association to which Ireland would belong.[16] That oath should be compared with the Treaty oath, which read:

> I . . . do solemnly swear true faith and allegiance to the Constitution of the Irish Free State as by law established, and that I will be faithful to H.M. King George V, his heirs and successors by law, in virtue of the common citizenship of Ireland with Great Britain and her adherence to and membership of the group of nations forming the British Commonwealth of Nations.

In both the Treaty oath and the one proposed by de Valera the first allegiance would be to the Irish constitution, and fealty would be sworn to the King in virtue of Ireland's association with Britain and the dominions, but each oath envisioned a different form of association. The Treaty oath involved common citizenship and dominion status, while the President had been thinking of External Association with reciprocal citizenship. He candidly admitted that he had no problem about swearing to be 'faithful' to the King. Instead of using the word *allegiance,* which was normally used in the case of one's sovereign, the word 'faithful' had been included in the Treaty in an effort to denote equality between those taking the oath and the monarch. 'I take it to mean that "faithful" is as regards a bargain made in the faithfulness of two equals who show it by keeping the bargain,' de Valera explained. His main difficulty with the Treaty oath, he said, was swearing 'allegiance to the constitution of the Irish Free State as by law established.' Since the Free State constitution would be established by British law in the name of the British King, he contended that anyone taking the oath would be swearing allegiance to the King.[17]

'The point is,' de Valera emphasised, 'that the oath contained in the Treaty actually and unequivocally binds the taker to "allegiance" to the English King, for under the terms of the Treaty the constitution of the Irish Free State "as by law established" is the King of England and nobody else.'[18] For instance, the constitution would be drawn up by a Provisional Government which, under the terms of the

Treaty, would be established by those elected to the Southern Parliament in accordance with the terms of the Partition Act. As the latter act was passed by Westminster in the name of the King, it would follow that the Free State constitution would in theory, at least, be drawn up in the King's name. Moreover, as it would be enacted by the British parliament in the name of the King, it would automatically follow that Westminster would have the same authority to amend the constitution. In theory, therefore, the British parliament would be legally empowered to interfere at will in Irish affairs in the name of the King, but such interference would, in effect, not only be unconstitutional but would also be a violation of the Treaty's stipulation that the Free State would have the *de facto* status of Canada and the other dominions. Although the King was still theoretically an absolute ruler, de Valera himself had publicly accepted that the Crown had long since ceased to enjoy that power, with the result that the King's authority was largely symbolic.

From the purely political standpoint, the President's candor would seem to have been a blunder because in clearly defining his objections to the Treaty, he nakedly revealed just how small those differences actually were, with the result that many people sided with Griffith and Collins on the grounds that the differences were not worth fighting for. The delegation had already failed to persuade the British to accept the proposals on the lines of Document No. 2, so Collins predicted that Lloyd George would not even listen if the Irish tried to re-open the negotiations.

The President agreed that it would be useless trying to get the British government to accept his proposals by conventional negotiations. 'No politician in England would stand by them,' he admitted. So he did not envisage sending a delegation at all but hoped to present his alternative as 'a sort of appeal to the two nations.'[19]

'It would be a document that would give real peace to the people of Great Britain and Ireland and not the officials,' he said. 'I know it would not be a politicians' peace. I know the politician in England who would take it would risk his political future, but it would be a peace between peoples, and would be consistent with the Irish people being full masters of everything within their own shores.'[20]

Some of de Valera's critics did not give due recognition to the differences that existed between the agreement and Document No. 2. In symbolic terms the two documents were significantly different. The symbolic links with the Crown and Empire were retained virtually intact in the Treaty, while Document No. 2 modified them greatly. Yet in the last analysis the President himself agreed that Ireland would have practically the same freedom under either system. 'It is right to say that there will be very little difference in practice between what I may call the proposals received and what you will have under what I may propose,' he declared. 'There is very little in practice but there is that big thing that you are consistent and that you recognise yourself as a separate independent state and you associate in an honourable manner with another group.'[21]

In admitting that, de Valera was consistent with his earlier views concerning the *de facto* status of the dominions, which he described as complete independence. Since Ireland was supposedly being accorded the same *de facto* status, it followed that she would also be independent but, of course, the President did not accept that conclusion. He thought that the British might exercise their *de jure* powers to deny that freedom to Ireland because of her closeness to them. In short, he did not believe that Britain would respect the Treaty.

Collins did not argue that the Treaty was perfect. 'In my opinion,' he said, 'it gives us freedom, not the ultimate freedom that all nations desire and develop to, but the freedom to achieve it.'[22] In other words, the agreement could be used as a stepping-stone to the desired independence. He believed that London would respect the Treaty because, as Smuts had pointed out during the summer, the dominions would have a vested interest in ensuring that Britain did not violate Irish sovereignty, as such a violation would set a precedent for similar interference in their own affairs. Thus under de Valera's alternative Ireland would lose the protection of the dominions without gaining any appreciable security because if Britain was going to violate the Treaty, then it would be easier to violate Document No. 2 as it would not move Ireland any further away from Britain. Consequently Collins genuinely believed that some aspects of the agreement were even better than Document No. 2.

In one respect, at least, de Valera eventually agreed. Some months later, he wrote privately that the Twenty-six Counties would, in effect, have a better chance of ending partition as a member of the British Commonwealth than if his alternative was implemented. While advocating that Republicans should act as if Document No. 2 was the Treaty, he nevertheless acknowledged that 'whilst the Free State were in supposed existence would be the best time to secure the unity of the country.'[23]

A number of suggestions were broached in an attempt to meet de Valera's objections, such as having the Dáil transfer the necessary authority for the Provisional Government to function. Although the Dáil and Southern Parliament were theoretically different institutions, they were the same in practice, as the Republican regime had used the elections for the Southern Parliament to elect the second Dáil in May 1921. The Dáil could therefore easily authorise the Provisional Government to draw up a constitution, and the Irish people could then claim that the Dáil, not the British King, had been the ultimate authority for the Free State Constitution. In that way the Irish side would not acknowledge the King as the source of the Free State's independence and Westminster would not, even by implication, be recognised as having the right to interfere in Irish affairs. If the Treaty came into force in that way, critics could evaluate the agreement in action without first having to surrender their principles.[24]

De Valera initially predicted that Griffith and Collins would not accept the idea, but on learning that they had responded favourably he rejected it himself.[25] He also dismissed comparatively similar suggestions put forward by both Collins and by a group of backbench members of the Dáil, including some of his own supporters like Seán T. O'Kelly and Paddy Ruttledge.[26]

During the debate the President did irreparable damage

to his reputation as a practical moderate by acting throughout the proceedings as if he had a right to determine Dáil procedure. He intervened repeatedly and spoke more than two hundred and fifty times during the thirteen days of public and private debate. Although many of those interruptions were admittedly only short interjections, some were quite lengthy. That he was allowed to interrupt so often no doubt testified to his standing within the Dáil, but his opponents did eventually become somwhat exasperated. He had been allowed to introduce Document No. 2 during the private session, and both Griffith and Collins complied at the ensuing public session with what they felt was his unreasonable request that his alternative not be mentioned after he had withdrawn it, but they balked when he tried to introduce a revised version of Document No. 2 as an amendment at the close of business on 4 January 1922. Having already agreed that no amendment could be entertained to the Treaty until the agreement had been first voted upon, de Valera seemed to be splitting hairs when he argued that he was not proposing an amendment to the Treaty but an amendment to the resolution calling for the Dáil's approval of the Treaty.

'I am responsible for the proposals,' he told a stunned Dáil, 'and the House will have to decide on them. I am going to choose my own procedure.'[27]

In a scathing editorial next day the *Freeman's Journal* accused de Valera of making a 'criminal attempt to divide the nation' by pressing 'an alleged alternative' that contained 'all the articles for which the Treaty had been assailed by the "ideal orators of Dáil Éireann".' The editorial contended that the President's own vanity was the real reason for his opposition to the London agreement.

Having been blocked in his efforts to introduce the amended version of Document No. 2, the President did not even try to use a hair-splitting technicality to justify reneging on the cabinet agreement not to resign until the Dáil had voted on the Treaty. On 6 January 1922 he announced his resignation to a packed house in the course of a speech in which he made the startling assertion that 'whenever I wanted to know what the Irish people wanted I had only to examine my own heart and it told me straight off.' After announcing his resignation he declared that the Dáil would have 'to decide before it does further work, who is to be the Chief Executive in this nation.'

'If you elect me and you do it by a majority,' he said, 'I will throw out that Treaty.' He added that he would appoint a new government which would then offer Document No. 2 'as a genuine peace treaty — to the British peoples, not merely Lloyd George and his government, but to all the States of the British Commonwealth.'[28]

This rather blatant attempt to have the vote on the Treaty turned into a personal vote of confidence in himself evoked so much criticism that the President soon withdrew his resignation on the understanding that the vote on the Treaty would be taken expeditiously.

Some people concluded that the real reason for de Valera's opposition to the Treaty was annoyance that he had not been called to London at the eleventh hour so that he could personally secure credit for the agreement. Although that assessment was an over-simplification, it was not wholly without substance.

His initial welcoming of the news that the Treaty had been signed showed that he was not primarily interested in being in on the actual signing, but he thought at the time that the British had agreed to External Association, and he could feel that he had been a principle architect of the settlement. On learning that the agreement did not contain all that he had anticipated, he opposed it and complained to the Dáil about the delegation's failure to consult him before signing. 'I was captaining a team,' he said, 'and I felt that the team should have played with me to the last and that I should have got the last chance which I felt would have put us over.'[29]

There was a remarkable similarity between de Valera's attitude during the Treaty controversy and his actions after his plank had been rejected at the Republican Party's National Convention in Chicago a year and a half earlier. When Cohalan managed to get a plank accepted that was couched in more politic terms, de Valera undermined it and revealed that although he knew no Presidential candidate would support his own resolution, he nevertheless planned to launch a propaganda campaign to convince enough Americans to support the resolution in the hope that one of the Presidential candidates could be persuaded to adopt it. Publicly he contended that he undermined the Cohalan plank on the principle that it understated the Irish case, but that was not true. Indeed he privately admitted that the real reason was to demonstrate that he, not the judge, was the spokesman for the Irish cause. He genuinely believed that Ireland would be best served if he was seen to be in charge of the movement.

Later, during the Treaty debate, the President concentrated on the unacceptability of the oath, which he depicted as a matter of principle on which he could not accept the agreement, but here again his actions were obviously not based on the principle he tried to depict. At one point during the secret session, he actually admitted that he might have accepted the Treaty oath earlier but would have said 'No' at the time of the signing because he believed it was possible to get better terms. 'I would have said "No",' he explained, 'though I might not have said "No" before. I would have said "No" in the circumstances because I felt that I could have said "No" with advantage to the nation.'[30] In essence, therefore, his opposition was a matter of tactics — not principle, as he ultimately demonstrated by subscribing to the oath in order to get back into the Dáil in 1927.

While the Dáil was considering the Treaty de Valera compared his opponents with the Cohalan faction. When Document No. 2 initially failed to secure sufficient support, he contended that it had been undermined by Collins working through the IRB in much the same way that Cohalan had worked through Clan-na-Gael. 'It was a case of Cohalan and his machine over again,' the President wrote.[31]

'What has sickened me most,' he told the Dáil towards the end of the public debate, 'is that I got in this House the same sort of dealing that I was accustomed to over in America from other people of a similar kind.'[32] Having come to look on Collins in much the same light as Cohalan, the President acted towards him in much the same way as he had towards the judge. It would seem that de Valera allowed his own attitude towards the Treaty to become significantly influenced by his determination to show that he — not Collins — was the real Irish leader, just as his attitude towards the Cohalan plank had been moulded by his earlier determination to show that he was the spokesman for the Irish cause, even in America.

For the Dáil to have accepted the President's suggestion that the Treaty be rejected and Document No. 2 presented to the British people instead would have been as foolhardy as he must have been naive if he believed that the propaganda campaign he advocated had any more chance of success than his similar effort to win over the American electorate in 1920 after the Chicago debacle. A successful campaign in 1922 would have needed the sympathetic understanding of at least some sections of the press, which there was little chance of securing, as the only organs opposing the Treaty had done so on the grounds that the agreement was too generous towards Sinn Féin. Not one Irish daily newspaper supported de Valera's position, and there was little prospect of getting international support because even American opinion was strongly in favour of the settlement.

Harry Boland, who returned from the United States in order to vote against the Treaty, admitted in the Dáil that 'the great public opinion of America is on the side of this Treaty,' and he added that the American press had adopted 'a unanimous attitude in favour' of it.[33] There was little sympathy for de Valera. In fact, the *New York Times* carried an editorial bitterly critical of him on the day the Dáil's vote was eventually taken:

> Apparently he essayed a Napoleonic or Cromwellian stroke in resigning, at the same time that he demanded re-election with all power placed in his hands; but when this failed, he talked and acted like a hysterical schoolgirl. Whatever happens in Ireland, de Valera seems to have hopelessly discredited himself as a leader. Narrow, obstinate, visionary and obviously vain, he has now, in his representative capacity, wrought immense harm to the Ireland of his professed

entire devotion.[34]

There was strong support for the Treaty even among de Valera's supporters in the United States. The President of AARIR had come out in favour of the agreement. In addition, Harry Boland had himself initially welcomed it. He praised the Treaty as 'an agreement which restores Ireland to the community of nations.'[35]

Boland afterwards explained that he issued that statement before the terms of the Treaty were published in the United States. Having been personally assured that nothing less than External Association would be acceptable, he said he had assumed the agreement was in line with the plan. On finding that such was not the case, he changed his mind and voted against the Treaty.

While Boland's explanation was understandable, it did not explain why, after the terms had been published, he actually denounced Cohalan and the secretary of FOIF for criticising the agreement.[36] The pair of them had ironically been among the first to criticise the Treaty publicly, but they subsequently supported it after they learned that de Valera was opposed to it. Such vicissitudes certainly lent credence to the view that personalities figured largely in stances adopted towards the Treaty.

In the Dáil the personality of Collins figured prominently at the conclusion of the debate. Brugha delivered a bitter personal tirade against him in winding up the case against the Treaty, and Griffith then jumped to the defence of Collins in winding up the whole debate on Saturday, 7 January 1922.

It was shortly after half past eight in the evening when the official announcement was made that the Dáil had voted in favour of the Treaty by 64 votes to 57. The historic moment passed without any sign of jubilation within the assembly. People sat in relative silence until word filtered out into the streets where hundreds of people had gathered. Then the wave of enthusiastic cheering that erupted outside seemed to stir the Dáil.

De Valera was the first to speak. 'It will, of course,' he said, 'be my duty to resign my office as Chief Executive. I do not know that I should do it just now.'

'No,' cried Collins from across the floor.

'There is one thing I want to say,' the President continued. 'This is simply approval of a certain resolution. The Republic can only be disestablished by the Irish people. Therefore, until such time as the Irish people in regular manner disestablish it, the Republic goes on.'

Collins, who had predicted shortly after signing the Treaty that he had signed his own death warrant, was keenly aware of the dangers ahead. 'In times of change,' he warned the Dáil, 'there are always elements that make for disorder and that make for chaos.' He suggested therefore that those on both sides of the house should 'form some kind of joint Committee' to preserve order.[37]

Reporters thought the President was about to respond favourably but Mary MacSwiney, the sister of the late Lord Mayor of Cork, spoke before he had a chance to respond. As she spoke, the *Freeman's Journal* reported, 'she seemed obsessed by a consuming rage.'[38]

'I, for one, will have neither hand, act, nor part in helping the Irish Free State to carry this nation of ours, this glorious nation that has been betrayed here tonight, into the British Empire,' she said. 'I maintain here now that this is the grossest act of betrayal that Ireland ever endured.'[39]

Whether, as reporters believed, the President was about to respond favourably to the suggestion made by Collins must remain a matter for conjecture. Possibly they were right, but few could have guessed then that they may well have been witnessing the first manifestation of de Valera's unwillingness to take a stand in the face of the irreconcilable bitterness of some of those on his own side. 'From this time,' according to one member of the Dáil, de Valera appeared 'in the role of a leader who did not lead, while forces which he could not control pushed the country steadily towards the horrors of civil war.'[40]

The President, instead of responding to Collins, simply called on those who had voted against the Treaty to meet with him the following afternoon. He was obviously marshalling his forces to bring the fight against the Treaty to the Irish people.

Collins renewed his appeal to those across the floor.

'Even though our physical presence is so distasteful that they will not meet us,' he said, 'some kind of understanding ought to be reached to preserve the present order in the country.'[41]

'I would like my last word here to be this,' de Valera responded: 'We have had a glorious record for four years; it has been four years of magnificent discipline in our nation. The world is looking at us now —.' At that point he burst into tears and collapsed sobbing into his chair. Women in the chamber were crying openly as were some of the men, while others were visibly trying to restrain their tears as the Dáil adjourned for the night.

Next day the anti-Treaty deputies decided to form their own organisation, *Cumann na Poblachta*, but they did little about it at the time other than agree upon its name. They concentrated instead on their next move in the Dáil. It was decided that de Valera should go ahead with his plans to resign the Presidency and then run for re-election. If successful, he would refuse to include in his cabinet any of those who had voted for the Treaty. They also decided that there 'should be no co-operation' with the efforts of pro-Treaty leaders to implement the Treaty, but that 'no action should be taken likely to lead to violence or civil war.'[42]

Nobody should have been surprised on Monday morning when de Valera formally announced his resignation in the Dáil. Collins, for one, anticipated the announcement. He immediately proposed the President be replaced by a committee of public safety consisting of representatives from both sides of the house until a general election could be held, but de Valera rejected the proposal, saying that it was unconstitutional. 'I have tendered my resignation and I cannot, in any way, take divided responsibility,' he declared. 'You have got here a sovereign Assembly which is the Government of the nation. This assembly must choose its executive according to its constitution and go ahead.'[43]

On being challenged to outline the policy he proposed to pursue in the event of being re-elected, de Valera explained he would 'carry on as before and forget this Treaty has come'. Once the Irish people understood the implications of the Treaty, he predicted they would not stand for it. 'I have perfect confidence in the people of the country,' he said, 'that when that Treaty is worked out in legislative form and put before them that then they will know what they have got; that then they will understand what they are doing by accepting this Treaty and not till then.'[44]

When his bid for re-election was criticised on the grounds that it tended to make a mockery of normal constitutional government by seeking to give power to the minority rather than the majority of the Dáil, de Valera defended his stand. 'I am thinking of it as the better and the constitutional and the right and proper way to do the work,' he said.[45] 'Remember, I am only putting myself at your disposal and at the disposal of the nation. I do not want office at all. Go and elect your President and all the rest of it. You have sixty-five. I do not want office at all.'[46]

Griffith delivered a cold and reasoned attack in which he depicted the President's proposition as a twisted appeal to the emotionalism of members in order to circumvent the Treaty. He noted, for example, that there was no need for the President to resign in the first place. 'We suggested that Dáil Éireann might continue until the Free State election came into effect,' Griffith explained. 'There is no necessity for him to resign today. His resignation and going up again for re-election is simply an attempt to wreck this Treaty.'[47]

The proposal to re-elect de Valera was debated into the late afternoon. Some supporters argued that as no other candidate had been nominated, he should be deemed elected unanimously. If the former President was simply concerned with retaining office, he could easily have done so by withdrawing his resignation. Instead, he was anxious for a vote, and refused to consider the idea of being returned to office by default.

'I cannot, naturally, stand for that,' he declared.[48]

Collins tried to nominate Griffith, but the Speaker ruled that the Dáil would first have to vote on the nomination of de Valera. When the vote was taken de Valera did not vote in an apparent effort to emphasise that he was not personally seeking office but only putting himself at the disposal of the nation. This could easily have been a very costly jesture, because he was defeated by only two votes, 60 to 58, with the result that had only one of those who voted against actually voted for him, his own vote would have made the difference between victory and defeat.

Griffith immediately rose to pay a generous tribute. The vote, he said, had not really been against de Valera; it was for the Treaty. 'I want to say now,' he added. 'that there is scarcely a man I have ever met in my life that I have more love and respect for than President de Valera. I am thoroughly sorry to see him placed in such a position. We want him with us.'

'I voted, not for personalities, but for my country,' shouted one deputy amid cries for order. 'Dev has been made a tool of and I am sorry for it.'

'I want to assure everybody on the other side that it was not a trick,' de Valera replied. 'That was my own definite way of doing the right thing for Ireland. I tell you that from my heart. I did it because I felt it was still the best way to keep that discipline which we had in the past.' Obviously mindful of the danger ahead, he continued, 'I hope that nobody will talk of fratricidal strife. That is all nonsense. We have got a nation that knows how to conduct itself. As far as I can on this side it will be our policy always.'[49]

The complexities of implementing the Treaty began to surface when Collins proposed Griffith as 'President of the Provisional Executive', rather than President of the Dáil or of the Irish Republic. Under the terms of the Treaty, it was not the Dáil, but the Parliament of Southern Ireland established under the Partition Act (1920), which would appoint a Provisional Government to take over the administration of the Twenty-six Counties from the British until the Treaty could be formally implemented. To a practically minded individual like Collins, this posed no problem. Members of the Dáil had been elected under the machinery set up for the home rule parliament, so all of its members — with the exception of one anti-Treaty deputy elected from a Northern Ireland constituency — were eligible to sit in the Southern Parliament, which Collins argued could be called by the Irish name, *Dáil Éireann*.

He was obviously trying to get around that objectional aspect of the Treaty which would have meant recognising Britain's right to legislate for Ireland. Collins believed this could be circumvented if the Dáil also authorised the Provisional Government to act for it. In that way the Irish side could always contend that the Provisional Government derived its authority from the Irish people, rather than the British crown.

De Valera was adamant, however, that the Dáil could not transfer any of its authority or do anything to implement the Treaty without the prior approval of the Irish people. In effect he was contending that from the British and Irish standpoints there would have to be two governments — the Dáil executive which would be recognised under Irish law, and the Provisional Government, which would take over the administration at Dublin Castle and thus be recognised under British law.

It was, of course, ironic that de Valera, of all people, should be so obstinate when the controversy centred on the actual title that the chief executive would use, as it was he who had changed the title from *Priomh Aire* to President back in 1919 without the authority of the Dáil, and without consulting any of his cabinet colleagues. In fact, he waited for more than two years before he had the constitutional position regularised with an amendment in August 1921. Thus it was paradoxical that he should object so strenuously to allowing Griffith to function for a few months under an adapted title, but more than a title was really at stake.

The wrangle over the title was left unresolved overnight, before Griffith conceded to de Valera's demands. 'If I am elected,' Griffith told the Dáil next morning, 'I will occupy whatever position President de Valera occupied.'[50]

'Hear, hear,' cried de Valera, who had won his point. 'I feel that I can sit down in this assembly while such an election is going on.' He changed his mind shortly afterwards and announced that he was walking out of the Dáil 'as a protest against the election as President of the Irish Republic of the Chairman of the Delegation who is bound by the Treaty conditions to set up a State which is to subvert the

Republic.'[51] Accompanied by supporters, the former President walked out amid some rather childish name calling.

Although de Valera returned to the Dáil later the same day, he left no doubt that he was not about to sit idly by while the Treaty was being implemented. 'We will continue every resistence against outside authority that has been imposed on the Irish people,' he told a press conference next day. 'We have a perfect right to resist by every means in our power.'

'Even by war?' asked a reporter.

'By every means in our power to resist authority imposed on this country from outside,' he replied.[52]

Meanwhile Griffith and Collins were arguing that the Treaty could be used as a stepping-stone to full independence. Indeed they wasted no time in giving a practical demonstration of their ability to circumvent British symbolism by having Griffith, in his capacity as chairman of the Irish delegation which negotiated the Treaty, summon the Southern Parliament to meet on 14 Janaury 1922. Under the terms of the Partition Act the Lord Lieutenant was supposed to convoke the session in the name of the crown and all members were supposed to take an oath of allegiance, but this was not taken. Thus, in a strict sense, Britain's authority was not recognised as Griffith derived his authority from the Dáil. Yet de Valera and his Republican colleagues still refused to attend the session, which elected Collins chairman of the Provisional Government. He in turn appointed a cabinet including most members of the cabinet appointed by Griffith. As a result the pro-Treaty people were involved in both the Dáil cabinet and the Provisional Government, and the difficulties caused by the dual arrangement were largely symbolic because most of the parallel posts in each administration were held by the same individuals.

De Valera nevertheless rejected the argument that the Treaty could be used as a stepping-stone to complete freedom. 'It is not a stepping-stone,' he told an American correspondent, 'but a barrier in the way to complete independence. If this Treaty be completed and the British Act resulting from it accepted by Ireland, it will certainly be maintained that a solemn binding contract has been voluntarily entered into by the Irish people, and Britain will seek to hold us to that contract. It will be cited against the claim for independence of every future Irish leader.[53]

In the following days Collins emphasised that the Free State Constitution, which was being drawn up by a committee of the Provisional Government under his own chairmanship, could give a further practical demonstration of the validity of the stepping-stone argument. He explained that the constitution could incorporate the clause that was at the very heart of External Association by stipulating 'the legislative, executive and judicial authority of Ireland shall be derived solely from the people of Ireland.' Collins also privately promised that the Treaty-oath prescribed for members of the Free State Parliament could be omitted from the constitution so that members would not have to take or subscribe to it.[54]

De Valera was, of course, highly sceptical. He challenged the pro-Treaty faction to make good its boast by framing the constitution and presenting it to the people so 'they would know what they were voting on.'[55] Although out of government, he was by no means in the political wilderness. He was still President of the Sinn Féin Party, and it soon became apparent that he enjoyed the support of the rank and file of a majority of party members, although the party's *Árd Chomhairle* was pro-Treaty. De Valera used his influence at the party's Árd Fheis, which convened on 21 February 1922, to extract an agreement from Griffith and Collins to delay the proposed elections for three months and to have the constitution published beforehand. In return he used his influence to have a resolution shelved which would have prohibited those who had voted for the Treaty from standing again as Sinn Féin candidates.

De Valera was initially content with the Árd Fheis agreement. He told a gathering in Ennis a few days later that they could reject the Treaty and then see if the Irish people were really being given a free choice. 'Use your free choice and vote for the Republic, which you know in your heart you want,' he said. 'We do not deny that there are dangers in such a course, but we ask you to brace yourself to face them. We do not deny that any more than we deny that there are certain advantages to be got immediately from the agreement that was signed, but they would be got at too great a price.'[56]

Within a fortnight, however, de Valera was demanding the electoral register be updated, which would have necessitated an even longer delay than the three months agreed at the Árd Fheis. 'The register on which you propose to hold the elections,' he wrote to Griffith, 'contains tens of thousands of names that should not be on it, and omits tens of thousands that should be on it — the latter mainly those of young men who have just attained their majority, who were the nation's most active defenders in the recent fight, and whose voice should certainly not be silenced in an election like the pending one, in which the fate of their country and the ideals for which they fought are to be determined.'[57]

Observing that it would take more than five months to complete a new register, Griffith was not prepared to agree to that kind of delay. He was obviously exasperated at the attitude being adopted by de Valera, who seemed impossible to satisfy. Every time some concession was made to him, he simply proceeded to make further demands, as if there had been no concession at all. When he demanded that the electoral register be updated after he had concluded the Árd Fheis agreement, it was not surprising that Griffith thought the former President was only looking for a political advantage by delaying the election rather than being concerned about the democratic rights of the unfranchised.

De Valera's actions in the following weeks certainly gave rise to grave doubts about his own commitment to democracy. On 15 March 1922 he formally launched *Cumann na Poblachta* and set out on a speaking tour. In Dungarvan next day he argued that the Treaty should be rejected and the fight with Britain continued. 'If you don't fight today,' he said, 'you will have to fight tomorrow; and I say when you are in a good fighting position, then fight on.'[58] The following day in Thurles he told a crowd, which included a contingent of armed IRA, that if the Treaty were ratified they would have 'to wade through Irish blood, through the blood of the soldiers of the Irish Government, and through, perhaps, the blood of some members of the Government in order to get Irish freedom.'[59]

Much to de Valera's annoyance, his speeches were widely interpreted as either threatening civil war or attempting to incite it. He indignantly refuted such suggestions. Indeed he felt that critics were using his words to do those very things of which they were accusing him. 'You cannot be unaware,' he wrote to the editor of the *Irish Independent,* 'that your representing me as inciting to civil war has on your readers precisely the same effects as if the inciting words were really mine.'[60]

De Valera certainly had a point, but it is difficult to avoid the conclusion that his speeches, even if intended only as a realistic assessment of the situation, were dangerous and irresponsible. 'The Irish people were only too well aware of the threat of civil war and needed no warnings about it,' according to Professor Joseph M. Curran. 'Certainly, excitable young men with guns in their hands did not need the kind of warning de Valera gave. For a leader of his stature to utter prophecies of bloody domestic conflict only increased its likelihood.'[61]

There was already a great deal of discontentment within the IRA. Most of the headquarters staff controlled by Collins and his IRB colleagues, were pro-Treaty, while divisional commanders and the rank and file volunteers were strongly anti-Treaty, especially in those areas which had been most active in the struggle against the British. Following his resignation as President de Valera had called on anti-Treaty troops to afford his successor the same allegiance given to himself, but this was too much for some of the more radical. 'It doesn't matter to me what he said,' Rory O'Connor, the Director of Engineering, declared. 'Some of us are no more prepared to stand for de Valera than for the Treaty.'[62] When O'Connor and others demanded that an Army Convention be called, Richard Mulcahy, the Minister for Defence, agreed but then reversed his decision after it became apparent that anti-Treaty elements would not only control the convention but would probably rescind the army's decision to pledge its allegiance to the Dáil.

Once it became apparent that the more militant segments of the IRA were unwilling to give their continued allegiance to the Dáil with its pro-Treaty majority, de Valera publicly suggested that the IRA should split on Treaty lines. 'I have sufficient faith in the Irish people to believe that they can divide without turning on one another,' he said, adding that it would be better to have two disciplined armies which were each united than one divided and powerless force.[63]

Many people actually thought that de Valera instigated the move when O'Connor — claiming to represent eighty per cent of the IRA — announced that the Army Convention would be held on 26 March 1922 in defiance of the headquarters staff and the President. At a press conference in the building where *Cumann na Poblachta* had its headquarters, O'Connor explained that the army had freely placed itself under the Dáil so it would be justified in reverting to its former status, as the Dáil had betrayed the Republic by recommending the Treaty. He added that 'the holding of the Convention means that we repudiate the Dáil.'

'Do we take it we are going to have a military dictatorship, then?' a reporter asked.

'You can take it that way if you like,' replied O'Connor.[64]

The convention, which was duly held three days later, was attended only by anti-Treaty representatives who elected an Executive of their own, thus splitting the IRA along Treaty lines. Under the new executive the anti-Treaty IRA, or Irregulars as they were widely known, became particularly active, conducting raids for arms and bank robberies to finance their operations.

Although de Valera 'heartily disagreed' with their actions, he was reluctant to take an open stand against them. Yet on 6 April 1922 he did reaffirm the right of the people to accept the Treaty.

'Everybody regards the will of the Irish people as supreme,' he told a gathering in Dun Laoghaire. 'I do for one. Not merely do I say I for one hold that this nation, taking away all force, should have the right to do with itself what it wants, but I would say further, that even in the circumstances of the moment — even with the threat of war — the Irish people would have the right even — if they wanted to do — to avoid war by taking another course.'[65]

His remarks were probably prompted by private misgivings about the actions of the Irregulars, especially their repudiation of the Dáil, but de Valera retreated from those sentiments within a matter of only a few days, as if the Dun Laoghaire speech had just been a temporary aberration. In an interview with John Steele of the *Chicago Tribune* that weekend he defended as natural the decision of the Irregulars to revert to the army's former independent status. 'If the Irish people were allowed a free choice,' de Valera added, 'they would choose by an overwhelming majority exactly what these armed forces desire.'[66]

The Irregulars, he explained in another interview, were 'entitled in the last resort to prevent elections such as those proposed which may well be regarded as the device of an alien aggressor for obtaining, under threat of war, an appearance of popular sanction for his usurped authority.'[67] He contended that the Irish people were not being denied their democratic rights by the Irregulars, but by the British Government. 'The threat of war from this government,' he declared, 'is intimidation operating on the side of Mr Griffith and Mr Collins as sure and as definite as if these gentlemen were using it themselves, and far more effective, because indirect and well kept in the background. Is our army to be blamed if it strives to save the people from being influenced by, and from the consequences of, giving way to this intimidation?'[68]

Griffith and Collins, on the other hand, held de Valera primarily responsible for the deteriorating situation. Speaking in Wexford over the weekend, Collins accused the former President of talking like a despot. 'And not the avowed despot,' he added, 'but of a more dangerous one — of the despot posing as a greater lover of liberty than other men, of the despot who shouts the name of liberty louder, while he tramples the form of liberty underfoot.' He went

## DE VALERA'S DARKEST HOUR

on to accuse de Valera of having used treasonable language.

'Was it by civil war, by shedding the blood of our brothers that we could win peace and freedom?' Collins asked. 'Can he not cease his incitements? They are incitements whatever may be his personal intention. Can he not strive to create a good atmosphere instead of seeking to create a bad one?'[69]

That same day in Cavan the President charged that de Valera had privately accepted there was no hope of securing British recognition of the Republic before the Irish delegation went to London the previous October. Observing that Lloyd George had made it clear that under no circumstances would the British negotiate on the basis of recognising the Republic, Griffith stated that de Valera had accepted that situation before the London Conference began.

Of course there was nothing new in that charge. Both Griffith and Collins had already repeatedly argued on those lines. Indeed, each of them had stressed the same points publicly in the Dáil during the Treaty debate. Now de Valera, with his influence seriously waning among the more radical Republicans, seemed particularly touchy about the suggestion that he had been less than firm on the Republican position. He reacted to Griffith's Cavan-speech by issuing an almost hysterical statement to the press:

> Of all the mean and barefaced falsehoods by which a needless and shameful surrender of a noble cause, a breach of a pledged word and of public faith, a turning of political coats, and of swallowing of principles, almost without parallel, is sought to cover up, there is scarcely any more brazen than this pretence that the independence and sovereignty of Ireland as enshrined in the Republic was abandoned before the Plenipotentiaries went to London, either by Dáil Éireann itself, or by the Cabinet of Dáil Éireann, or by me.[70]

It was not just the war of words that was heating up. Dublin awoke on Good Friday, 14 April 1922, to find that overnight the Irregulars had seized some prominent city centre buildings, including the Four Courts, where they established their headquarters. The similarity with the start of the Easter Rebellion six years earlier was unmistakable. Although O'Connor and his men had not even informed, much less consulted de Valera, it was still assumed that the latter had a real influence over them. A delegation from the Labour Party therefore turned to him that day in an effort to diffuse the situation.

'We spent two hours pleading with him, with a view to averting the impending calamity of civil war,' one member of the deputation later recalled. 'The only statement he made that has abided with me since as to what his views were was this: "the majority have no right to do wrong". He repeated that at least a dozen times in the course of the interview, in response to statements made to him to the effect that the Treaty had been accepted by a majority, and that, consequently, it was his duty to observe the decision of the majority until it was reversed. He refused to accept it on the ground that the majority has no right to do wrong.'[71]

Some years later de Valera explained his attitude: 'What appeared to be an obvious wrong was being justified by the idea that it was backed by the majority vote of the people. I said that that did not justify wrong. That never justified wrong. If you got a unanimous vote of the people telling you to go and shoot your neighbour, you would be quite in the wrong in carrying out that majority will. You would not be right. Therefore the majority rule does not give to anybody the right to do anything wrong, and I stand by the statement.'[72]

In the purely abstract sense he was correct, but he had not been talking in the abstract in April 1922. Taking his remarks within their proper context, there could be no doubt that de Valera was contending that the Irregulars had the right to ignore the wishes of the majority of the Irish people. If his words were actually twisted, as he would later have had the people believe, then he must take the responsibility for not clarifying his statement so that it would not be so open to such misrepresentation.

On Easter Sunday, he issued an inflamatory proclamation, which ended with an emotional appeal to the young

## DE VALERA'S DARKEST HOUR 109

people of the country. 'Young men and young women of Ireland,' he declared, 'The goal is at last in sight. Steady; all together; forward. Ireland is yours for the taking. Take it.'[73]

In view of the occupation of the Four Courts and other prominent buildings only three nights earlier, the proclamation was naturally interpreted as de Valera's way of encouraging young people to support the Irregulars. He certainly gave no public indication that he was actually critical of what those people were doing.

The Roman Catholic Archbishop of Dublin tried to avert the impending civil war by inviting de Valera, Brugha, Griffith and Collins, together with some Labour leaders, to a conference at the Mansion House, but it proved virtually impossible to make progress in the face of the enormous personality differences that had developed among the Sinn Féin leaders, as each faction believed the other was guilty of treachery.

At one point Brugha accused Griffith and Collins of being British agents. The archbishop immediately intervened to have the remark withdrawn. Brugha agreed, but went on to explain that he considered those who did the work of the British Government as British agents.

Collins was infuriated. 'I suppose,' he said, 'we are two of the ministers whose blood is to be waded through?'[74]

'Yes,' replied Brugha quite calmly, 'you are two.'

For months the most vile accusations were being hurled against Griffith and Collins, while de Valera stood by in apparent indifference, depicting himself as having consistently tried to maintain the Republican position. He never denied that he had been prepared to compromise with the British, but he contended that he had insisted that the country would always, in effect, be a republic.

'Was that your attitude?' Griffith asked. 'If so a penny postcard would have been sufficient to inform the British Government without going to the trouble of sending us over.'

When de Valera tried to explain, Griffith interrupted. 'Did you not ask me to get you out of the straight-jacket of the Republic?'

'Oh, now, gentlemen, this won't do any good.' cried the archbishop, no doubt mindful of de Valera's somewhat hysterical comments in the press little over a week earlier.

'I would like to explain,' de Valera said, 'because there is a background of truth to the statement.' He had obviously asked Griffith for help, but he was undoubtedly thinking of the straight-jacket of the isolated Republic. There was so much bitterness between Griffith and Collins on the one hand, and de Valera and Brugha on the other, that the two sides had to withdraw to separate rooms while the others tried to mediate, but it proved impossible to reach an agreement.

Few people realised at the time that de Valera was largely impotent when it came to negotiating on behalf of hardline Republicans. 'If de Valera were on your side,' Mary MacSwiney wrote to Richard Mulcahy on 24 April 1922, 'we should still fight on. We do not stand for men but for principles, and we could no more accept your Treaty than we could turn our backs on the Catholic Faith.'[75]

She was in for a rude awakening a couple of days later, however, when the Roman Catholic hierarchy issued a blistering condemnation of the 'immoral usurpation and confiscation of the people's rights' by the Irregulars 'who think themselves entitled to force their views upon the nation.' The bishops added that the dispute over which was supreme, the Dáil or the Provisional Government, mattered little because the two bodies were in practice the same, in view of their overlapping personnel. The hierarchy's statement concluded that 'the one road to peace and ultimately to a united Ireland, is to leave it to the decision of the nation in a general election, as ordered by the existing Government, and the sooner the election is held the better for Ireland.'[76]

The Irregulars were determined nevertheless to prevent the election, and de Valera publicly supported them. From a purely democratic standpoint there were indeed valid reasons for opposing an election on an outdated register with the British threatening war if the Treaty were not approved. The British were actually using their threat to bolster support for the Treaty. Winston Churchill, who as

Colonial Secretary was charged with dealing with Irish affairs, wrote at the time, that 'the more the fear of renewed warfare' was present in the minds of the electorate, the more likely they were 'to go to the polls and support the Treaty.'[77]

De Valera rejected several suggestions that Griffith and Collins put forward to prevent intimidation at the polls. They even offered to arrange a referendum in which all adults could participate — whether on the electoral register or not. The people would meet at the same time in designated localities throughout the country and then vote by passing through barriers, where they would be counted. But de Valera flatly rejected the use of such 'stone-age machinery'. He objected, moreover, to the fact that the referendum would only be held in the Twenty-six Counties, instead of throughout the island. In addition to the objections he had already voiced about holding elections on the outdated register or under the British threat of war, it was noteworthy that he also publicly justified his refusal to co-operate on the grounds that there were 'rights which a minority may justly uphold, even by arms, against a majority.'[78]

The former President proposed that the issue of the Treaty should not be referred to the people for a further six months. 'Time would be secured for the present passions to subside,' he explained, 'for personalities to disappear, and the fundamental differences between the two sides to be appreciated, the work of national reconstruction begun, and normal conditions restored.'[79]

'We all believe in democracy,' de Valera told a correspondent of the *Chicago Tribune* shortly afterwards, 'but we do not forget its well-known weaknesses. As a safeguard against their consequences the most democratic countries have devised checks and brakes against sudden changes of opinion and hasty, ill-considered decisions.' In the United States a treaty needs the approval of a two-thirds majority of the United States Senate. As the Irish system had 'not yet had an opportunity of devising constitutional checks and brakes,' de Valera seemed to suggest that the Irregulars were not only justified in refusing to accept the decision of the majority of the Dáil but also right in taking the initiative in trying to prevent an election in which the Treaty would be an issue. 'The Army sees in itself the only brake at the present time,' he said, 'and is using its strength as such.'[80]

For one who had posed for years as a champion of the right of self-determination, de Valera seemed to be drifting into an untenable position, as he was obviously trying to paper over the differences between his own political wing of the anti-Treaty side and the Irregulars on the military wing. It was especially important that those differences should be minimised as the anti-Treaty position was already hardpressed on the propaganda front.

'The propaganda against us is overwhelming,' de Valera wrote to a friend in the United States. 'We haven't a single daily newspaper on our side, and but one or two weeklies. The morale of the people seems to be almost completely broken, but that was only to be expected when the leaders gave way. Still I trust we may be able to bring things right again.'[81]

Having previously rejected overtures to play a part in setting up an administration back in January, de Valera seemed to change his mind on 17 May 1922. 'I would like to ask the President and Ministers on the other side a straight question,' he said in the Dáil. 'Do they or do they not want our co-operation in the government of Ireland at the present time?'[82]

The former President contended that the only authority in the country had been established by the Irish people and any other authority (i.e. the Provisional Government) was a pretended authority with no validity in Ireland. 'But,' he added, 'if the Irish people, or the representatives of the Irish people, so desired they could use any machinery set up by that authority for Ireland's benefit and that in so far as it was necessary for the representatives of the people to use that, they were entitled to use that without departing from fundamental principles.'[83] In essence, he was saying that he was prepared to co-operate with the Provisional Government in matters advancing the cause of Irish freedom but would not foresake any fundamental principles which were contradicted by the Treaty.

Collins, who had pleaded with de Valera to adopt such an attitude both before and after the Dáil voted on the Treaty, thought that the former President was now only trying to save face. After further talks between them they agreed on 20 May 1922 to an election pact. In accordance with the pact, which was ratified by the Dáil, the two wings of Sinn Féin would put forward a united panel of candidates in proportion with their existing strength in the Dáil, and if elected, they would form what would amount to a coalition government with portfolios being allocated on a five to four ratio in favour of the pro-Treaty wing, while the Defence Minister would be elected by the army. In short, the Treaty would not be an election issue at all.

On learning of the arrangement, the British were furious. Churchill demanded an explanation of the pact, which he considered both undemocratic and a violation of a provision in the Treaty which stipulated that every member of the Provisional Government had to signify acceptance of the Treaty. Admitting that the anti-Treaty people would likely be unwilling to signify such acceptance, Griffith nevertheless defended what Collins had done as a means of actually advancing the Treaty.

'Does it matter if de Valera is in charge of education?' Kevin O'Higgins asked the British. 'Are we bound to take steps which would wreck the Treaty?'[84]

Collins argued that agreeing to the pact was the only way the election could be held, because the Irregulars would otherwise disrupt the balloting. If nothing else, he contended, the agreed election, in which other candidates would be free to oppose Sinn Féin, would undermine the argument then being used by de Valera and others that the existing Dáil had been elected on a platform to uphold the Irish Republic and did not therefore have the authority to implement the Treaty. If the Irish people elected a pro-Treaty majority, this would be tantamount to endorsing the agreement.

Having mollified Churchill's fears about the pact, Collins tried to use the election deadline to rush the British into accepting a constitution which would be in line with Document No. 2. The draft document excluded the Treaty-oath and incorporated an autochthony clause stipulating that 'the legislative, executive, and judicial authority of Ireland shall be derived solely from the Irish people.' There was also a clause stipulating that only the Free State parliament could declare war on behalf of the country. Since the British parliament had to pass the Irish constitution, this was tantamount to acknowledging the Free State's right to neutrality, which was the prized right de Valera had contended would make 'a clean sweep' of the whole defence question during the Treaty negotiations.[85]

Although the British accepted most of the provisions, they balked at the exclusion of the oath. Its omission, they insisted, was a violation of the Treaty. Having pressed hard for its exclusion, Collins finally relented. The oath was therefore incorporated into the constitution and the Treaty itself was also scheduled to the document with the stipulation that in any matter where there was a conflict between the Treaty and the constitution, the former would take precedence.

The text of the constitution was only released on the eve of the election, with the result that the Irish people did not have a chance to see it until published in the daily press on election day. This, of course, effectively denied critics the chance of explaining the document before polling. Thus while the constitution had been published in accordance with the strict terms of the Árd Fheis agreement, de Valera and others could hardly be blamed for thinking that the timing had not been faithful to the spirit of that agreement, nor could they be criticised for holding that Collins had also been unfaithful to the spirit of the election pact because during a public meeting in Cork just two days before the election, he seemed to suggest that the people should vote for other candidates rather than support anti-Treaty candidates on the Sinn Féin panel.

'I am not hampered now by being on a platform where there are coalitionists, and I can make a straight appeal to you, to the citizens of Cork, to vote for the candidates you think best of, whom the electors of Cork think will carry on best in the future the work that they want carried on,'

Collins said. 'You understand fully what you have to do, and I will depend on you to do it.'[86]

By implication, at least, those remarks seemed to be a violation of the pact. But it should be noted that the anti-Treaty faction had already violated the pact in many instances by using intimidation to prevent independents and the candidates of other parties from contesting the elections.

Polling day was 16 June 1922 and though Sinn Féin had deliberately avoided making the Treaty an election issue, there could be no doubt that the people favoured the pro-Treaty segment of the party. Of the 65 pro-Treaty candidates, for example, 58 were elected, while only 35 of the anti-Treaty people were successful. Even those figures exaggerated the anti-Treaty support, because 16 of the anti-Treaty candidates were returned without opposition. Where the seats were contested, 41 of 48 pro-Treaty candidates were successful, which was over 89 per cent, while only 19 of 41 anti-Treaty candidates were elected, amounting to barely 46 per cent. The popular vote painted and even bleaker picture for the anti-Treaty side, which received less than 22 per cent of the first preference votes cast, and only just got second place ahead of the pro-Treaty Labour Party, which won 17 of the 18 seats it contested, and in the process secured only 1,353 less first preference votes than the combined total of the anti-Treaty side, which fielded more than twice as many candidates. As a result there could be no doubt that the Irish electorate favoured accepting the Treaty — at least as a short-term measure.

Nevertheless some of the Irregulars had no intention of accepting any such verdict. Two days after the election, they held another convention at which it was proposed that their Executive should give the British seventy-two hours notice of the termination of the Truce and restart the war with Britain. Although twelve of the sixteen-man Executive supported the motion, it was vigorously opposed by the Chief-of-Staff, Liam Lynch, and also by Cathal Brugha. When a ballot was taken, the proposal was narrowly defeated by 118 votes to 103.

Rory O'Connor and others refused to accept the decision. They returned to the Four Courts, where they admitted only those who had supported their unsuccessful motion. The twelve dissident members of the Executive then repudiated Lynch and elected a new Chief-of-Staff of their own, Joe McKelvey.

De Valera played no part in the machinations of those in the Four Courts. He concentrated instead on political matters, especially the unacceptability of the proposed constitution. 'As it stands, it will exclude from public service and disfranchise every honest Republican,' he declared. 'Dáil Éireann will not dishonour itself by passing it.'[87] At the time he confidently expected to be a member of the new cabinet in line with the pact agreement. The whole political climate was upset when two members of the IRA assassinated Field Marshall Sir Henry Wilson outside his London home on 22 June 1922. This sparked a chain of events that were to have tragic consequences for the nation and all involved.

The British, believing that those in the Four Courts were responsible for Wilson's murder, demanded that the Provisional Government should clear out the building without delay. Churchill announced in the House of Commons that pressure was being exerted on Dublin to end the occupation:

> If it does not come to an end, if through weakness, want of courage, or some other even less creditable reason it is not brought to an end, and a speedy end, then it is my duty to say, on behalf of His Majesty's Government, that we shall regard the Treaty as having been formally violated, that we shall take no steps to carry out or legalise its further stages, and that we shall resume full liberty of action in any direction that may seem proper. . .[88]

While those in the Four Courts apparently had no involvement in Wilson's murder, the Republicans nevertheless forced the pace of events when on 27 June they raided the premises of a Dublin car dealer and seized sixteen cars to be used to send a convoy to the Six Counties. Authorities of the Provisional Government managed to arrest some of the raiders, but those in the Four Courts retaliated by kidnapping the deputy Chief-of-Staff of the Provisional Government's army. It was this act which finally prompted Collins to clear out the Four Courts, although in view of Churchill's statement some people, not unnaturally, concluded that the British had forced the decision.

An ultimatum was issued to the garrison in the Four Courts to withdraw by the early hours of 28 June 1922, and when the time limit expired, the forces of the Provisional Government began a bombardment with guns borrowed from the British. This has generally been considered the start of the civil war.

In view of de Valera's more inflamatory remarks in recent months, he was held largely responsible for the conflict. He had, however, really tried to lead the more radical elements of his supposed followers on a sane path. For example, he called for Army unity, he denounced talk of civil war, and he demanded the Irish people be consulted on the Treaty which, he contended, they had a right to accept even under the British threat of war. But militant Republicans were unwilling to follow his lead in any of these matters, so de Valera backed down on each of them. He called for the Army to divide on Treaty lines, talked rather recklessly about the danger of civil war, and demanded the postponement of the elections. In his own mind those changes were justified as a desperate effort to regain his waning influence among the radicals in order to avert the calamity of civil war. He was trying to lead supposed followers who were not prepared to take their lead from him. On several occasions he, in effect, ran out in front of them and proclaimed where they should go, only to find that they would march on in a different direction. By repeating this process, he was actually following the militants as they brought the country down the road to civil war.

CHAPTER FIVE

# All the Public Responsibility

## *The Civil War*

Having learned of the assault on the Four Courts, de Valera lost little time in issuing a statement condemning the actions of the pro-Treaty forces. 'At the bidding of Englishmen,' he declared, 'Irishmen are today shooting down, on the streets of our capital, brother Irishmen — old comrades in arms, companions in the recent struggle for Ireland's independence and its embodiment — the Republic.' He added that those in the Four Courts 'would most loyally have obeyed the will of the Irish people freely expressed, but are not willing that Ireland's independence should be abandoned under the lash of an alien government.' Consequently he called on the Irish people to rally to their assistance. 'Irish citizens, give them support! Irish soldiers, bring them aid!'[1]

The former President then enlisted in the Irregulars and eventually joined those occupying the Gresham Hotel on O'Connell Street. In spite of press reports to the contrary, he was never one of the recognised military leaders, although he did take an active part in trying to stop the hostilities. After the fall of the Four Courts his comrades in O'Connell Street were prepared to stop fighting and allow the whole issue to be settled by the Dáil, which was due to meet on 30 June 1922, but their offer was ignored.

De Valera sent messengers to both Griffith and Collins, whose response was to insist that the men surrender their weapons. 'Let them lay down their arms,' the pro-Treaty leaders insisted, 'and then we'll talk to them.' The former President thought this attitude was most unwise. 'Had the offer been accepted,' he later contended, 'the whole civil war would have ended with the Four Courts incident and terms would have been arranged before the war had properly commenced.'[2]

Griffith and Collins were apparently determined to force the Irregulars into line once and for all. The Dáil was prorogued until 15 July 1922, much the chagrin of de Valera, who later characterised the action as a *coup d'etat*.

While the Irish people had undoubtedly supported the Treaty at the polls, this did not mean that pro-Treaty elements of Sinn Féin were given *carte blanche* to proceed as they wished. They had no authority either to postpone the Dáil, or to demand that the Irregulars surrender their weapons, any more than the President of the United States could deny Americans their constitutional right to bear arms. In all likelihood Griffith and Collins could have persuaded the Dáil to pass legislation denying the Irregulars the right to keep their weapons, but this was not done. Instead, Griffith and the members of the Provisional Government, who actually constituted a minority within the third Dáil, took it upon themselves to ignore the assembly and act without its authority.

The inaugural session of the third Dáil, which was postponed on three occasions, did not convene until after members of the Labour Party threatened to resign their seats. They had become frustrated at the undemocratic activities of those whom de Valera characterised as a ruling junta. Without consulting the majority of elected representatives, W. T. Cosgrave took over as chairman of the Provisional Government from Collins in mid-July and as acting President a fortnight later following Griffith's death. De Valera had no doubt that his opponents were acting illegally. They had never asked for his nominees to the new cabinet, as they should have done in accordance with the Pact, which was legally binding as it had been ratified by the Dáil.

Nevertheless it was de Valera who was publicly saddled with the brunt of the responsibility for the civil war, as the press characterised him as the real leader of the Irregulars, although he actually had little influence with their leadership. 'The newspapers,' he complained, 'are as usual more deadly to our cause than the machine guns.'[3] One pro-Treaty organ charged that de Valera had not only flouted the democratic principle of majority rule in refusing to accept the majority decision of either his cabinet, the Dáil, or the Irish people, but had also 'incited neurotic young men and emotional young women to set aside a principle which governs the politics of every civilised country, and drove them to make war on their own people under the pretext of "maintaining the Republic", which he himself abandoned.'[4]

Shortly before the fall of the Gresham Hotel became imminent, de Valera, who was particularly critical of 'the very foolish type of battle' in which the Irregulars had become engaged, slipped out of the building and managed to make his way south to Munster, most of which was under Republican control. But by late August the Irregulars, who were no match in conventional warfare with their enemy, which enjoyed an almost unlimited supply of British weapons, were dislodged from all their major strongholds, and it was obvious that they would have to resort to guerrilla tactics if they were to continue the struggle.

De Valera became preoccupied with the thought of arranging peace. He had no doubt that the majority of the people were critical of the Republicans. 'In Fermoy, Mallow, and other towns, the people looked at us sullenly, as if we belonged to a hostile invading army,' Robert Brennan recalled. 'Dev had seen all this, as had I, and that was one of the reasons he was so desperately trying for peace while he still had some bargaining power.'[5] One of those who met the former President at the time thought 'he seemed a man heartsick and distraught at the terrible things which had come to the nation and its people.'[6]

Many good men had fallen. Brugha had been killed, as had Harry Boland. On the other side Griffith had died — his death no doubt hastened by the strain of overwork. De Valera spoke kindly of the dead President, but was fearful that Collins, who had taken over as Commander-in-Chief of the Regular forces, would try to set up a military dictatorship.

'Any chance of winning?' de Valera asked himself. If there was a possibility, he felt that the Republicans had a duty to press on. But if there was no real chance, then he thought it his duty to persuade 'the men to quit — for the present'. He was definitely inclined towards quitting, because he was convinced that the Irish people would have to be won over 'to the cause before any successful fighting can be done.'[7]

'Dev says we "should surrender while we are strong",'[8] Childers wrote home, but Liam Lynch, who had again become the undisputed Chief-of-Staff of the Irregulars following the fall of the Four Courts, had no intention of surrendering. Warning that de Valera was trying to end the war, Lynch urged his Deputy Chief-of-Staff, Liam Deasy, not to give the former President any encouragement.

De Valera met Deasy in Gurranereagh, some four miles from the tiny County Cork village of Béalnabláth on 21 August 1922. 'We discussed the war situation far into the night,' Deasy later recalled. 'His main argument was that, having made our protest in arms and as we could not now hope to achieve a military success, the honourable course was for us to withdraw.' Deasy concurred to a certain extent with that line of reasoning but pointed out that the majority of the men 'would not agree to an unconditional cease-fire.'[9]

Next morning Deasy accompanied de Valera to the cross at Béalnabláth, where they learned that Collins had just passed through the area. When the former President asked what local Irregulars were likely to do, Deasy predicted that an ambush would be prepared in the event that Collins returned by the same route. One of those present then remarked that Collins might not leave his native county alive.

'I know,' replied de Valera, 'and I am sorry for it. He is a big man and might negotiate. If things fall into the hands of lesser men there is no telling what might happen.'[10]

Next day de Valera learned that Collins had indeed returned by the same route and had been killed in the ensuing engagement. The former President did not share the elation of the man who brought him the news. 'It's come to a very bad pass,' he said, 'when Irish men congratulate themselves on the shooting of a man like Michael Collins.'[11] It seemed as if he momentarily forgot that he personally held Collins largely responsible for the civil war.

Collins must indeed share some of the blame for the conflict, because in his efforts to avoid it, he compromised himself by trying to do the impossible. He worked tirelessly to placate both the Republicans and the British. His fault was that he tried to do too much and in the process made contradictory commitments he could not possibly keep, thereby opening himself to the charge of insincerity. Professor T. Desmond Williams concluded that both de Valera and Collins were largely to blame for the civil war because, he wrote, 'Collins tried to do too much, and de Valera too little.'[12]

Yet once the fighting began the former President did try to persuade his side to stop fighting. Having failed to persuade both Lynch and Deasy, he asked for a meeting to be arranged so that he could talk with the whole Irregular Executive, but Lynch refused to call the meeting, much to the irritation of de Valera, who went so far as to meet secretly with Collins' successor, Richard Mulcahy, on 6 September 1922. According to Mulcahy, the former President explained that he neither agreed with what was being done, nor had any responsibility for it, but added that the leaders on his side believed what they were doing, so he would follow them as a humble soldier as long as they continued. De Valera was trying to find some kind of basis for peace in a revision of the Treaty, but Mulcahy insisted that the terms of the Treaty were not negotiable.[13]

The former President was despondent. 'We have,' he wrote to Joe McGarrity, 'all become involved in the most hateful of conflicts — civil war — in which there can be no glory and no enthusiasm, unless one allows himself to be mastered by the spirit of party or faction. Worst of all, there seems to be no way out of it. I am convinced that there is the will for peace on both sides, but no basis is discoverable on which it can be made.'[14]

'I have often taken myself to task,' he added, 'but I do not see what I could have done which would have averted this war. The May Pact with Collins provided a bridge by which the forces of the nation could be brought together again and united against the common enemy if that was his purpose, and a constitutional way out if he was determined to stick to his Treaty policy.' De Valera went on to accuse his opponents of being 'guilty of every sort of unconstitutional and illegal action,' but stressed that the fundamental question was still 'the Treaty or not the Treaty?' On that, he admitted, 'we are in a minority.'

He was on the horns of a dilemma:

> If the Republicans stand aside and let the Treaty come into force, it means acquiescence in the abandonment of the national sovereignty and in the partition of the country — a surrender of the ideals for which the sacrifices of the past few years were deliberately made and the sufferings of these years consciously endured.
>
> If the Republicans do not stand aside, then they must resist, and resistance means just this civil war and armed opposition to what is undoubtedly, as I have said, the decision of the majority of the people.
>
> For Republicans the choice is, therefore, between a heartbreaking surrender of what they have repeatedly proved was dearer to them then life and the repudiation of what they recognise to be the basis of all order in government and the keystone of democracy — majority rule.
>
> Is it any wonder there is, so to speak, a civil war going on the minds of most of us, as well as in the country (where we have brother actually pitted against brother)?[15]

When the third Dáil eventually convened on 9 September 1922 de Valera was in a quandry. He was apparently hoping to attend the session when he passed through Béalnabláth a fortnight earlier, but he had since changed his mind and decided to stay away for reasons 'of principle and expediency'.[16] He felt justified in abstaining on principle, because the dual set-up of the Dáil cabinet and the Provisional Government was being abandoned and the two amalgamated on the grounds that the Irish people had endorsed the Treaty in the June election. This ignored the fact that the Treaty was not supposed to be an issue at the time. It was also a blatant violation of the Pact ratified by the Dáil, which alone had the right to repeal the provisions of the Pact. In ignoring the Pact, therefore, the cabinet acted illegally.

From the standpoint of expediency, on the other hand, de Valera felt that it would be best if Republicans stayed away from the Dáil not only because the divisions within their own ranks would become exposed but also because they could not be effective in the assembly, as they would be greatly outnumbered.

'Our presence at the meeting would only help to solidify all other groups against us,' he wrote. 'We would be the butt of every attack. We could not explain — we would be accused of obstructing the business and "talking" when we should "get on with the work".' Thus the presence of Republican representatives would 'not promote but retard peace'. Nevertheless he thought it best not to explain publicly his absence, or that of his Republican colleagues, but to keep the other side 'guessing as to the reason for the present.'[17]

De Valera was personally toying with the idea of repudiating the Dáil and setting up a Republican government instead. He felt that the Irregular Executive could justifiably contend that the new Dáil was 'an illegal assembly in as much as it was summoned by the illegal junta called the "Provisional Government".'[18] Since the second Dáil had not met as it should have after the June elections in order to dissolve formally before the third Dáil convened, Republicans could contend that the second Dáil was still the country's legitimate parliament, and he saw positive political merits in such an approach.

'This is much more positive and much better than a mere abstention of the Republican members,' de Valera advised, 'and if we are to be consistent at all it is the attitude we should adopt. We will be at sixes and sevens with one another, I think, if any other policy is adopted. I favour it accordingly.'[19] Yet he vacillated for some weeks before adopting the policy.

Some Irregular leaders actually issued a public appeal calling on Republican members of the Dáil to meet separately as the legitimate parliament. Even if it proved impossible to muster the necessary quorum of twenty members, they argued that the requirement could be fulfilled by deeming any deputy who was prevented from attending to be present 'in spirit'.[20]

'This is no use,' de Valera declared. It was not, of course, that he disliked the idea of setting up a Republican Government at the time, but he was afraid that it would not be possible to sustain it. 'I have opposed the setting up of a rival Government solely because of obvious inability to maintain it,' he wrote. 'If we were now in the position we were when we held a portion of Cork, I'd certainly favour it. But again we cannot maintain it. If the Army Executive were at hand and would definitely give allegiance to the Government, I'd think it wise to try it — but again the inability to maintain it.'[21]

Unless the Irregular Executive was prepared to give unconditional allegiance to the proposed Republican Government, de Valera felt that such an administration 'would be a farce'. The problem was that in repudiating the Dáil the previous spring the Irregulars had really repudiated all political control. 'Rory O'Connor's unfortunate repudiation of the Dáil, which I was so foolish as to defend even to a straining of my own views in order to avoid the appearance of a split,' de Valera explained, 'is now the greatest barrier that we have.' He added, moreover, that even if the Republican politicians secured the allegiance of the Irregular Executive, they sitll would not have the strength to make their will effective, because they could not, 'as in the time of the war with Britain point to authority derived from the vote of the majority of the people.' Under the circumstances he favoured the idea of transferring the whole responsibility for the struggle to the Irregulars. 'We, as a political party,' he wrote, 'should cease to operate in any public way — resign in fact.'[22]

'This is the course I have long been tempted to take myself,' he added, 'and were it not that my action might prejudice the cause of the Republic, I'd have taken it long since. Our position as public representatives is impossible.'

Lynch's refusal to arrange a meeting for him with the members of the Executive was exasperating to de Valera, who complained that 'the position of the political party must be straightened out. If it is the policy of the party to leave it all to the army, well, then the obvious thing for members of the party to do is to resign their positions as public representatives. The present position is that we have all the public responsibility and no voice, and no authority.' He was so annoyed at the existing set-up that he actually threatened to resign. 'If I do not get the position made quite clear,' he declared, 'I shall resign publicly.'[23]

'I am almost wishing I were deposed,' de Valera explained to McGarrity, 'for the present position places upon me the responsibility for carrying out a programme which was not mine.' The Irregulars were seeking to destroy the Treaty and all that it stood for, while de Valera only wanted to revise it. 'The programme "Revise the Treaty" would be mine,' he added, 'and I would throw myself into it heart and soul. I am convinced it is the only way for the present to keep the Republican idea alive.'[24]

Realising that the armed struggle would likely fail, de Valera was already thinking along the lines that he would use with considerable success during the following years. 'If the Free State should become operative, and the present physical resistance fails,' he wrote, 'I see no programme by which we can secure independence but a revival of the Sinn Féin idea in a new form. *Ignoring England.* Acting in Ireland as if there was no such person as the English King, no Governor-General, no Treaty, no oath of allegiance. In fact acting as if Document [No.] 2 were the Treaty. Later we could act more independently still. Whilst the Free State were in supposed existence would be the best time to secure the unity of the country. That is my one hope out of the situation. If we can get a single state for the whole country, then the future is safe.'[25]

Notwithstanding some public protestations to the contrary, there was only a small difference between the Treaty and what de Valera wanted, as epitomised by Document No. 2. Yet even during the civil war he still stood by his alternative steadfastly. 'I would make peace under present conditions, or any conditions I think likely to prevail in the immediate future, on the basis of that Document,' he wrote in mid-October 1922, 'and I do not want the young fellows who are fighting for the Republic to think otherwise. So that if I am challenged at any time as to whether I would accept that Document, I can only answer "Yes".'[26]

He was not sanguine, however, about the chances of getting such a settlement. For one thing he did not think the men who were doing the fighting would agree with him. 'My views and theirs as to the terms on which peace might be made,' he wrote, 'is unlikely to be the same and any difficulties under that head in the future would be far more disastrous even than the present.' He did not believe that 'any body but the Army Executive would now get the allegiance of the men who are fighting.'[27]

Previously he had been contending that any Republican government established with the 'unconditional allegiance' of the Army would be 'a farce', but he changed his mind when the need to be able to claim some kind of legitimate authority became apparent after the Roman Catholic hierarchy denounced the Irregulars on 10 October 1922. The bishops condemned the Irregulars for waging 'what they call a war, but which, in the absence of any legitimate authority to justify it, is morally only a system of murder and assassination of the national forces.' The hierarchy, which called for the virtual excommunication of all those fighting on the Republican side, made a strong appeal to the people to support the government. 'We desire,' the bishops declared, 'to impress on the people the duty of supporting the national Government, whatever it is, to set their faces resolutely against disorder, to pay their taxes, rents, and annuities, and to assist the Government in every possible way to restore order and establish peace.'[28]

De Valera responded by trying to set up a Republican government. He proposed that the Irregular Executive should call upon him 'to resume the Presidency and to form a government which shall preserve inviolate the sacred trust of National Sovereignty and Independence.'[29]

Privately de Valera emphasised that he was primarily interested in just setting up a government rather than trying to regain power himself. 'I do not care what Republican Government is set up,' he declared, 'so long as one is — only I will not take responsibility if I do not get the corresponding authority to act in accordance with my best judgment. If the Army think I am too moderate, well let them get a better President and go ahead.'[30]

On 25 October 1922 de Valera and six members of the second Dáil met secretly in Dublin to set up an 'Emergency Government'. They elected him President, and he appointed a twelve member Council of State that was supposed to advise the cabinet, which he would subsequently select. After the meeting a statement was issued announcing that de Valera had resumed the Presidency because the Provisional Government had joined in 'a traitorous conspiracy' designed to subvert the Republic by 'pretending to establish a so-called Free State and a Provisional Partition Parliament, creatures and subordinates of an alien legislature.'

One of the first acts of the Republican Dáil was to call on de Valera to protest formally to the Vatican 'against the unwarrantable action of the Irish hierarchy in presuming and pretending to pronounce an authoritative judgment' on a political question as to 'whether the so-called Provisional (Partition) Parliament, set up under threat of unjust war by a *coup d'etat,* was the rightful legislature and Government of the country or not.'[31]

In the following weeks de Valera and members of his cabinet issued a series of proclamations renouncing all debts contracted by the Provisional Government, rescinding the Dáil's approval of the Treaty, outlawing the existing courts, and announcing that anyone using them would 'be deemed an enemy of the Republic.'[32]

'I would have saved our people all this agony if I could and have proceeded by slower, but in my opinion surer stages,' de Valera wrote, 'only the Treaty side left me no opportunity. I have made up my mind that there is no way now but to *cut* the knot. There is no chance of opening it. This way too in the long run will be the way of least suffering for the nation.'[33]

Few people could really have been impressed by the proclamations, because the Emergency Government was surrounded by an air of utter unreality. It was, for instance, supposed to be advised by the Council of State, but the latter was unable to meet because many of its members were arrested before they could reach Dublin. Moreover some of his cabinet choices were already in jail, but de Valera selected them anyway because he wanted them to be regarded as nominally filling the positions.

'Organising the work here,' he complained to a friend in America, 'is extremely difficult, and *we are sorely in need of funds.*' In addition, some very good people who sympathised with Republican aims were refusing to help because they did not wish to become involved in fighting their fellow countrymen against the will of the majority of the people.[34] Thus in order to enlist their active support it would be necessary to win over the Irish people, but the press was so hostile there was little chance of getting the Republican message across to them. 'Poor "people",' de Valera wrote, 'how one begins almost to despair of democracy when one realises how little of the truth is allowed to reach them and how misleading the information on which they must form their judgments.'[35]

During November 1922, there were a couple of dramatic events which potentially seemed to afford real propaganda opportunities to educate the people. One of those events was occasioned by Mary MacSwiney going on hunger strike to protest against her imprisonment. As her ordeal would progress, comparisons would inevitably be drawn with the stand taken by her late brother the Lord Mayor of Cork, Terence MacSwiney, who had received enormous publicity for the Irish cause back in 1920 when he died after a protracted hunger strike in protest against his imprisonment by the British. Of course, once she began her fast it was vital that she continue, or else her protest would prove counterproductive. De Valera therefore urged her in the strongest terms to persevere:

> When Terry was dying, knowing how conscientious he was and how good, I feared that he might have some scruples about what he was doing, and intended giving him an official *order* to continue, as I might to a soldier running great risk on the battlefield. For him to surrender having begun would have been not *personal* defeat, but defeat for his cause. Your case is the same and may the God of Calvary give your spirit the neces-

sary strength to endure to the last if need be and take you to Himself when your ordeal is ended.[36]

The propaganda potential of her protest was enhanced after eleven days when her sister, Annie, went on hunger strike herself outside the gates of Mountjoy Jail, but before the whole protest was able to capture public imagination, the Provisional Government released Mary MacSwiney and transferred her to hospital. She had won, but her victory was almost completely overshadowed by other events which occurred during her three-week fast.

Back in October the Cosgrave government had announced an amnesty for all Republicans who gave up the fight; but at the same time it revealed that legislation recently passed would be enforced making the unauthorised possession of firearms a capital offence. On 10 November Childers was captured in possession of a small pearl-handled revolver which had ironically been given to him by Collins. 'The gun he had in his possession,' de Valera wrote, 'was an automatic that Mick gave, telling him to defend the Republic. I saw it myself — a tiny automatic, little better than a toy and in no sense a war weapon.'[37]

Nobody had yet been executed, so de Valera was not at first worried, although he did think it prudent to engage counsel for the defence. Believing 'the trial would educate our people as nothing else would,' he was confident that the Irish people would not tolerate 'the eternal disgrace' of consenting to the execution of Childers. 'I shall,' de Valera wrote, 'despair of our people if they stand by and see a champion of the dark days murdered by slaves at England's bidding.'[38]

'They may ill-treat him,' de Valera wrote to Molly Childers on 15 November 1922, 'but I do not think they will dare execute him.' That confidence was seriously shaken two days later, however, when four Irregulars were executed for possessing firearms. Later the same day Childers went on trial before a military tribunal. His defence, which claimed that he should be treated as a prisoner of war, emphasised that he was not recognising the right of the tribunal to try him. The defence counsel then with-

## DE VALERA'S DARKEST HOUR 131

drew. Next day Childers was duly found guilty and sentenced to death.

De Valera decided that Childers should appeal although this meant affording *de facto* recognition to what were legally the Crown courts of the Provisional Government. 'These wretches,' he declared, alluding to the members of Cosgrave's cabinet, 'are now desperate, and cruel with the cruelty of desperation, and they have by their infamous propaganda so prepared the way for the dark deeds they contemplate that it is necessary to dispute every inch of the way with them by every available means. Erskine's name is so much better known than any of the others that the case will rouse *the conscience* of all the best of our people and the case of an unknown would be passed over in silence and not reach them.'[39]

Although the subsequent appeal — unlike the trial — received extensive press coverage, it lasted only four days. The court rejected the defence contention that the military courts were illegally constituted, and it then dismissed the appeal itself on the grounds that 'once a state of war arises, the civil courts have no jurisdiction over the acts of the military during the continuance of hostilities.'[40] With those words the fate of Childers was sealed. He was executed early the following morning.

De Valera felt the execution keenly. He had lost the colleague for whom he had most respect. 'Of all the men I have ever met Childers was the noblest and the *best*,' he wrote to his wife, Sinéad. 'I have never met a man with whom I would have changed personalities except him and I only wish I could hope for as high a place in heaven as I am sure he will occupy.'[41]

One particularly infuriating aspect of the execution was the injustice of picking on Childers who, de Valera felt, was in 'no way responsible' for the civil war. 'Well may God forgive them,' the Republican President exclaimed. 'I would not like to let myself write what I feel.' Although he had himself been thinking in terms of surrendering only weeks earlier, he now displayed a distinct hardening of attitude. 'We must win now,' he declared. 'I am glad that we have the Government formed before this. It is so much easier to die for a definite positive programme.'[42]

There was no sign, however, that those 'best' people who were standing on the sidelines were moved by the execution to become actively involved, as de Valera had predicted. 'It is terrible,' he wrote the following week, 'to see how hard it is to get the people to give up the stupid policy of seeking the foreigner's leave to do what we have the right to do *and can do* without his leave.'[43]

Lynch reacted to the executions by warning that unless Irregular prisoners were properly treated in future, his men would 'adopt very drastic measures' to protect themselves.[44] In the following weeks and months, as reprisals met with counter-reprisals, the war plumbed even more inhumane depths than during the Black and Tan period.

On the day after the Irish Free State formally came into being on 6 December 1922, the Irregulars shot two members of the Dáil as a reprisal outside the Ormond Hotel. The Free State government then retaliated next morning by summarily 'executing' four of its more prominent Republican prisoners — Rory O'Connor, Joe McKelvey, Liam Mellows, and Dick Barrett, all of whom had been held without trial since the fall of the Four Courts. The following week the Irregulars reacted by burning the homes of some Dáil members and in the process killed the young son of one deputy.

This was too much for de Valera, who thought the reprisal tactics were proving counter-productive. 'The policy of an eye for an eye is not going to win the people to us and without the people we can never win,' he complained to Lynch. 'The recent burnings were, in my opinion, puerile and futile from a military or any other point of view.'[45] While holding that it was perfectly legitimate to burn Free State offices, de Valera drew the line at burning family homes. 'Terrorist methods may silence those of our opponents who are cowards,' he wrote, 'but many of them are very far from being cowards, and attempts at terrorism will only stiffen the bold men among them. I am against such methods on principle, and believe we will never win in this war until we attach the people to our Government by contrast with theirs.'[46]

At the time he believed the only hope the Republicans had of victory was to win over a large segment of the Free State Army, or else secure the overwhelming support of the people. Hence he was very conscious of matters showing Republican forces in an unfavourable light. He did not want to tie their hands in defending themselves against what he believed was the outrageous behaviour of their opponents. 'But,' he warned Lynch, 'the other side is dragging us and the country step by step into the mire with itself. I want to break the vicious circle somewhere, if I can.'[47]

Nevertheless the reprisals continued. On 11 February 1923 the father of Vice-President Kevin O'Higgins was shot at his home in front of his wife and teenage daughter. The killing seemed indicative of the desperation of the Republicans, who had suffered a serious pyschological set-back in late January with the capture of their Deputy Chief-of-Staff, Liam Deasy, who then signed a document calling on all his colleagues to agree to an 'immediate and unconditional surrender'.[48] This appeal, which was circularised to Lynch, de Valera and others, was published when no response was forthcoming. With the Republican position apparently crumbling de Valera's determination to salvage something from the struggle became more apparent. He not only rejected Deasy's call but even asked Lynch to order an acting member of the Emergency cabinet to leave Dublin before doing further damage with defeatist talk about the country being unwilling 'to fight anymore'.[49]

'Some of our good men are falling by the way,' de Valera wrote to McGarrity. 'The critical moment here has just arrived. Both sides are strained to the utmost, but I think we can bear it better than our opponents can, tho' at this very moment we received the biggest blow we have got since we started. If they find it doesn't knock us out they will despair, I think. Already they are divided into a war party and a peace party, almost of equal strength, I am told. We are a far more homogeneous body than they are. If this war were finished Ireland would not have the heart to fight another war for generations, so we must see it through.'[50]

In view of the Deasy affair, which was apparently 'the biggest blow', alluded to in the letter to McGarrity, it was important that Republican forces should dispel the impression that they were on the verge of collapse. Therefore de Valera enthusiastically supported an Irregular plan to launch a campaign of sabotage in Britain. 'Were we to abandon the Republic now,' he wrote, 'it would be a greater blow to our ideals and to the prestige of the nation, than even the abandonment on December 6th 1921. In taking it upon ourselves to be champions of this cause we have incurred obligations which we must fulfil even to death.' He therefore advised Lynch to make sure that the initial operation in Britain was a big concerted one followed by a series of other blows.[51]

Just as in the Black and Tan period de Valera was obviously thinking in terms of having the military campaign conducted in such a way as to exert political pressure on the other side to seek a negotiated settlement. He was actually confident that with public support from abroad the Republican side could achieve success. 'We are at the critical stage now,' he wrote to J. J. O'Kelly, a Republican emissary then in the United States. 'If our friends everywhere made one big effort we could win and smash the others. It must be death or glory for us now.'[52]

Throughout the struggle the Republicans had been receiving very little international support. Instead they were confronted with an extremely hostile press. On 24 January 1923 an absurd story received coverage on both sides of the Atlantic about Bolsheviks supposedly being behind the Republicans. 'Moscow is pouring into Ireland money, arms and propaganda,' the story went. 'The bellows of communism are blowing into a fiercer flame the dying embers of Sinn Féin, and the desperate faction is easily persuaded that fortune and power await them in a Soviet Republic.'[53]

De Valera tried to counter the unfavourable publicity by communicating with foreign correspondents. In one interview, published in the *Daily Mail* (London) on 3 February 1923, he predicted that the Free State was doomed. 'It is only in the cities and large towns that it has any life,' he said. 'The country districts are Republican. No state so founded can last long.' His optimism was not just a front for public consumption, as he also expressed similar views privately, such as in his letter to J. J. O'Kelly, which was quoted earlier, or in almost identical terms in a letter to McGarrity. 'One big effort from our friends everywhere,' he wrote, 'and I think we would finally smash the Free State.'[54]

While there was no military evidence to justify such optimism, de Valera was really thinking in terms of the political situation. On 7 February he wrote to Lynch suggesting that they try to find a constitutional settlement: 'It has always been my view that with anything like good will on both sides a constitutional way out of this impasse could be found. We can best serve the nation at this moment by trying to get the constitutional way adopted.' De Valera added that the Republican side should take the 'lead in this peace matter' as the whole country was so interested. 'If we make a decent peace offer, which will command the support of reasonable people, the others can't proceed and we shall have a victory.'[55]

Free State authorities were indeed coming under very strong political pressure to sue for peace. A few months later Lionel Curtis, a British cabinet secretary, reported that Cosgrave told him the 'worst moments had been in February' when some senators had 'shown a tendency to buckle, and had come to tell him that he must make terms with de Valera.' The President, however, remained resolute.[56]

'De Valera hopes to bring about negotiations which will enable him to make a dignified escape from his present position,' Cosgrave declared publicly at the time, 'but we are not going to help anybody in that way.'[57] Indeed Vice-President O'Higgins had already made it clear that the government was determined to pursue its campaign with vigour. 'The people who continue to act with Mr de Valera in his criminal conspiracy against the life and future of the Irish nation,' O'Higgins said, 'will have no cause for complaint if the Irish nation, acting on its instincts of self-defence and self-preservation, deals with them in a very summary and very ruthless fashion.'[58]

De Valera was thinking of issuing a personal statement suggesting that disputed issues be submitted to a vote of the Irish people, provided Free State authorities first agreed that the sovereign rights of the nation be fully recognised and all the nation's governmental powers be acknowledged as being derived exclusively from the Irish people. The will of the majority of the people would then form 'the ultimate court of appeal' for deciding any national issue in dispute — not because the majority would necessarily be right or just, but because this would afford a peaceful, democratic alternative to force.

But de Valera's plans for a peace initiative were frustrated by Mary MacSwiney, who insisted that he did not have the authority to make proposals without the approval of the Irregular Executive. She was adamantly opposed to accepting the principle that the people be recognised as the ultimate court of appeal. 'If that is granted,' she complained, 'our civil war has no sanction; the bishops are quite justified; and so is everything the F[ree] S[taters] have said to us. And if it is right now to submit to majority rule on this point, it was equally right last July. What have all the lives been lost for?'[59]

Confronted with this hardline opposition, de Valera backed away from his initiative. The following week, he actually stressed reasons why Republicans could not submit disputed issues to the Irish people when he answered some questions posed by a correspondent of the International News Service. 'When you submit a matter to a court,' de Valera explained, alluding to the court of public opinon, 'it is implied that you bind yourself by the decision of that court.' He then proceeded to list four reasons why Republicans could not accept a democratic decision of the people of the Free State: (1) the people had no right to vote away any part of the national heritage, as it belongs to 'all the generations'; (2) the whole thirty-two counties of Ireland should be consulted — not just the twenty-six of the Free State; (3) the vote would not be a free one so long as the British threat remained; (4) the Republicans had no means of getting their views across to the people because the press was so hostile. 'One cannot submit to the judg-

## DE VALERA'S DARKEST HOUR

ment of a court which cannot be informed of the facts,' de Valera concluded.[60]

Although frustrated in his efforts to launch a new peace initiative, de Valera did nevertheless resurrect his Document No. 2. 'The way to peace is to remove the threat of war,' he explained to a representative of the Press Association. 'Let England signify her willingness to accept the proposals which I put forward as an alternative to the "Treaty", January a year ago, and if there are any who prefer the "Treaty", let the Irish people decide as between the "Treaty" and these proposals.' Although some Republicans were not satisfied with his Document No. 2, he expressed confidence that they would not resist it in arms. He added that he was personally prepared to sponsor his proposals 'as a basis of an honourable peace' at any time. 'The fact that these proposals, and my statements, have been "twisted by knaves to make a trap for fools" doesn't take away from the truth that is in them,' he declared.[61]

De Valera was certainly in an unenviable position. 'I have,' he wrote, 'been condemned to view the tragedy here for the last year as through a wall of glass, powerless to intervene effectively.'[62] His opponents were holding him responsible for the civil war, while some on his own side were frustrating his efforts to secure a negotiated settlement. On the political front Mary MacSwiney was insistent that he secure the approval of the Irregulars for his new peace proposals, while on the military front, Lynch was refusing to convene the Army Executive for fear it would be persuaded to sue for peace.

Even the reference to Document No. 2 was resented by Lynch, who complained that the publicity surrounding it had 'a very bad effect' on the Republican soldiers and should therefore have been avoided. 'Generally they do not understand such documents,' he warned de Valera. 'We can arrange peace without referring to past documents.'[63]

Deeply irritated by the rebuke, the already frustrated Republican President began showing distinct signs of testiness. 'I will take no further responsibility for publicly handling the situation,' he wrote to Lynch, 'if I have, at every turn, to account for what I say, to people who have not given a moment's thought to the whole question.' Many good men had already come to the conclusion there was no hope of gaining their objectives, he continued, 'and if you were to hold that the objective was the "isolated" Republic, I would say they were right.'[64] He also wrote a rather frank, insulting letter to Mary MacSwiney. In it de Valera complained that while she tended to overestimate Republican strength and underestimate that of the Free State, he tended to do the opposite. 'Of the two,' he continued, 'I have no doubt that an omniscient being would rate my error as but a very small fraction of yours — vanity?'[65] It was ironic that he should, in effect, assume the insight of an omniscient being to suggest that somebody else was guilty of vanity!

The military position meanwhile continued to deteriorate with the Republicans. Their plans for a campaign of sabotage in Britain were undermined when their people were rounded up and deported to the Free State, where they were interned for the duration of the conflict. At the same time Free State forces were acting in the 'very summary and very ruthless' manner that O'Higgins had talked about some weeks earlier. On 7 March 1923, they took nine Republican prisoners and tied them to the stump of a tree in which a mine had been placed at Ballyseedy Cross, near Tralee. The mine was then detonated, killing eight of them. By some explosive freak one of the prisoners escaped to relate the story. The bodies of the others were so mutilated that the perpetrators of the deed did not realise that all nine had not been killed. There was a relatively similar incident involving five men the same day near Killarney, but again one man survived to tell the tale. As a result the following week in Cahirciveen Free State troops shot five prisoners in each leg to make sure they could not escape before blowing them up with a mine. This time one of their own colleagues was so disgusted that he defected and told the story. The war had degenerated to depths of depravity unknown in the Black and Tan period.

Lynch was no longer able to resist calls for a meeting of the Army Executive. When it eventually convened in the

Waterford mountains on 23 March 1923, de Valera had to suffer the indignity of being kept outside for three-quarters of an hour while those inside argued whether or not to admit him. On being admitted it was made clear to him that he would have no vote, but he was allowed to speak in favour of a motion advocating that continued resistance would 'not further the cause of independence.'[66]

Lynch, on the other hand, still believed that victory was possible, and he managed to have the motion defeated by six votes to five. De Valera was nevertheless authorised to investigate prospects of securing a peace which would not be inimical to his own announced principles. The Executive meeting then adjourned until 10 April 1923. In the following days Free State authorities were approached but they showed no interest in any of the peace overtures. They were determined to win the war. O'Higgins had declared recently that the government was determined that the war was 'not going to be a draw with a replay in the autumn.'[67]

De Valera, who began making arrangements for the reorganisation of the Sinn Féin Party, was firmly convinced that the Republicans should quit the armed struggle and turn to political methods. 'To me our duty seems plain, to end the conflict without delay,' he wrote to Paddy Ruttledge on 9 April. 'Those who would continue working for our independence must gird themselves for a long patient effort of renegotiation and education.'[68]

The same day Lynch was shot and fatally wounded, so the Executive meeting was postponed. Although de Valera professed an emotional preference for continuing the struggle, he contended that this would not be justifiable in the circumstances. 'I am afraid,' he wrote, 'we shall have to face the inevitable sooner or later, bow to force and resort to other methods, either ourselves or those to whom we leave the future of the cause.'[69]

Publicly, however, he tried to give a very different impression in an address to Republican forces. 'It is better to die nobly as your chief has died than live like a slave,' de Valera declared, adding that their cause was immortal — 'defeats may defer but cannot prevail against its ultimate triumph.'[70] He was obviously hoping that by appearing determined he might force the Free State government to seek a negotiated settlement, for fear the war would drag on indefinitely.

On 27 April 1923 de Valera was finally able to put forward the terms he had wanted to offer back in February. He publicly offered to call off the Republican campaign on condition that the sovereign rights of the nation were recognised as 'indefeasible and inalienable' with all legitimate legislative, executive, and judicial authority being derived from the Irish people, who would be 'the ultimate court of appeal'. He further stipulated that no citizens should be debarred from the government or parliament because of a refusal to take an oath. As a good-will gesture, he announced that all Republicans were being ordered 'to suspend all aggressive actions'. The order was due to come into effect not later than noon on the last day of the month.[71]

Next day de Valera met two senators, Andrew Jameson and James Douglas, with a view to having them act as intermediaries. They contacted Cosgrave, who authorised them to present the Free State's terms, which were that the Republicans should accept that all issues should 'be decided by the majority vote of the elected representatives of the people,' and that the Republicans should surrender their weapons. In return all military actions against them would be suspended and they would be free 'to canvass for the votes of the people at the next general election, provided they undertook to adhere strictly to constitutional action.' The senators reported that Cosgrave would not negotiate with the British regarding the oath, and the Republicans would have to subscribe to it, if they were to sit in the Free State Dáil.[72]

Cosgrave's terms were basically liberal. He later explained that he was not trying to humiliate the Republican side. He did not actually want the arms but was insistent that they should be given up. 'I am not interested in them,' he reportedly stated. 'They can be delivered up to a bishop anywhere. Let them be burned, but these arms cannot, and will not, if I have any responsibility for the government of this country, remain in the hands of those who are

## DE VALERA'S DARKEST HOUR

not subject to the authority of the people's parliament.'[73]

De Valera rejected those terms. The question of surrendering arms had been the very issue on which his peace efforts had foundered when he was in the Gresham Hotel at the start of the civil war, and he had always insisted that the oath was one no conscientious Republican would be able to take. If he surrendered on those issues now, it would mean that the whole civil war had been for nothing. He therefore re-issued his terms on 7 May 1923 with the added stipulation that pending an election, a suitable building would be furnished in each province where 'Republican arms shall be stored up, sealed up, and defended by a specially pledged Republican guard — these arms to be disposed of after the elections by re-issue to their present holders, or in such other manner as may secure the consent of the government then elected.' In publishing those terms the anti-Treaty weekly, *Éire,* noted that the conditions 'were intended simply as a basis for discussion.'[74] Cosgrave, who insisted that his government's terms were not negotiable, was immovable.

Some years later de Valera contended that the intransigence was personally motivated in order to ensure that he would not be able to get back into public life himself. 'It is a terrible thing to think,' he said, 'that men could be animated in big things by such mean motives.'[75]

In mid-May de Valera outlined the situation for the Army Executive and the available members of his Emergency Government at a meeting in a north Dublin suburb. He explained that Cosgrave was recalcitrant so they had the alternative of either surrendering to the Free State unconditionally, or else just dumping their weapons and quitting the fight without any surrender. He favoured the latter course and those present agreed with him.

The new Chief-of-Staff, Frank Aiken, therefore simply ordered the Irregulars on 24 May 1923 to dump their arms and accept that their enemies had 'for the moment prevailed'. At the same time de Valera issued a statement explaining that there was no longer any hope of military success. 'Further sacrifice of life,' he declared, 'would now be vain and continuance of the struggle in arms unwise in the national interest and prejudicial to the future of our cause. Military victory must be allowed to rest for the moment with those who have destroyed the Republic.'

The struggle now moved back into the political arena from which de Valera — notwithstanding some of his own public pronouncements to the contrary — had never really believed it should have strayed. He again came to the fore on the Republican side. Obviously he still thought the best way of achieving the ultimate Republican objectives was to pursue the policy he had outlined to McGarrity back in September 1922, which was before he had set up the Emergency Government. He now apparently had misgivings about retaining the Emergency arrangement. 'I have,' he wrote, 'been thinking whether it would not be possible to devise some scheme by which the real power of the nation would reside in some assembly outside any kind of parliament elected by their F[ree] S[tate] machinery, but I do not think anything of the kind is feasible.'

'The one policy that has a chance of success,' he explained, was:

(a) Maintaining that we are a sovereign state and ignoring as far as possible any conditions in the 'Treaty' that are inconsistent with that status — a policy of squeezing England out by a kind of boycott of Gov. General, etc.
(b) Breaching the 'Treaty' by the oath, smashing thro' that first and then compelling England to tolerate the breaches or bring her to a revision which would lead to something like the Doc[ument No.] 2 position.[76]

Since the Republicans had not surrendered nor accepted the Free State's terms, they were still liable to arrest, therefore de Valera had to stay 'on the run' and rely on issuing statements to the press in order to get his message across to the public. In one such statement on 28 June 1923 he announced that Sinn Féin candidates would contest the next general election to 'give the people an opportunity to put on record by their first preference votes their detestation of allegiance to a foreign king, their repudiation of partition, and their desire for a government which would really be obedient to their own will, and not an instrument of British domination.' He contended that the overall implications of the Treaty were still far from clear to the Irish people. Because of the civil war, the Boundary Commission had not yet met, nor had the financial issue — consideration of which had been postponed during the Treaty negotiations — been finally settled. Consequently de Valera argued that the people had 'not yet come to realise the humiliation of it all.'[77]

'But,' he added, 'they soon will. The fate of the North-East boundary clause and the amount of Ireland's share of the Imperial burden will be determined sometime. When it is, and the boundary clause has been waived, or some new ignominious bargain has been struck to evade it, and when, in addition, the full weight of an Imperial contribution of some ten to fifteen millions annually is being pressed upon their shoulders, the people will surely wake up, become conscious of the full extent of the deception that has been practised upon them, and learn what it is that those who gave their lives to prevent the consummation of this "Treaty" hoped to save them from.'

In a letter to the press some weeks later de Valera explained that three basic matters had been left unsettled in the Treaty. Those were the Free State's constitution, the Boundary Commission, and financial matters. 'What the "Treaty" implied with respect to each of them,' he wrote, 'was clear to any intelligent man or woman who gave it thought and attention, but the Irish people depended on the statements made by the press and their elected representatives who should have been their guardians. The "Treaty" advocates and the press immorally deceived them by the statements made in advance with regard to the Constitution, and then saved themselves by a scandalous political trick — publishing the Constitution on the morning of the poll. The attempt is now being made to cheat them on the Boundary Commission question and the financial settlement.'[78]

After Cosgrave called a general election, de Valera gave an interview to an American correspondent emphasising that the Republicans were serious about adopting a political approach. 'It is not the intention,' de Valera said, 'to renew the war in the autumn or after the elections. The war, so far as we are concerned, is now finished.'[79]

'We intend to devote ourselves to social reform, and to education, and to developing the economic and material strength of the nation,' he added. 'Politically we shall continue to deny the right, and to combat the exercise, of any foreign authority in Ireland. In particular we shall refuse to admit that our country may be carved up and partitioned by such an authority.' If Sinn Féin won a majority in the election, he said that his government would refuse 'to co-operate with England in any way until England was ready to make with us an arrangement as would make a stable peace possible — that is, an arrangement consistent with independence and unity of our country and people as a single state.'

Although de Valera had virtually ignored the partition issue during the Treaty debate in the Dáil, he was now raising it with increasing emphasis in his public statements — and not always with candor. The same day as his interview with the American correspondent, the *Irish Independent* was carrying a letter he had written to the editor implying that the partition clauses were under discussion when Griffith made the famous promise not to sign the Treaty, whereas in fact the issue in question had been in connection with the British Crown. Moreover, in the same letter to the editor, de Valera went on to state that he had 'never been able to understand' how Griffith had 'allowed himself to be deluded by the Boundary Commission idea',[80] which was a little disingenuous, seeing that de Valera had not only accepted the same scheme himself but had actually incorporated it almost *verbatim* when he introduced Document No. 2 in the Dáil.

While de Valera was trying to get Republicans to adopt a political approach, Free State authorities were not making things any easier for him. Indeed they seemed determined to frustrate him. On one occasion, Cosgrave and Desmond FitzGerald were campaigning in Tralee when someone in the crowd shouted, 'What about de Valera?'

'De Valera,' replied FitzGerald, 'is on the run, because he acted as an enemy of this country. As long as we are in power de Valera and every other enemy of the country will

## DE VALERA'S DARKEST HOUR                           145

have to be on the run.'[81]

Next day de Valera reacted by issuing a press release asserting that he and his colleagues had no intention of remaining in hiding indefinitely. 'Living or dead,' he declared, 'we mean to establish the right of Irish Republicans to live and work openly for the complete liberation of our country. Our opponents make a mistake if they imagine that we are going to remain on the run. If the people of Clare select me as their candidate again I will be with them and nothing but a bullet will stop me.'[82]

The Sinn Féin organisation in Clare duly invited de Valera to stand as a candidate for election, and he accepted. He announced that he would address a public meeting in Ennis on 15 August 1923. By coming out in the open he realised that he would highlight the fact that the struggle was being moved into the political arena. He was, of course, only too well aware of the dangers involved. If he fell into the hands of Free State troops his life would undoubtedly be in danger. Only recently, for instance, Noel Lemass, brother of the future Taoiseach, had disappeared having been arrested. (Some months later his body was found in the Dublin mountains.)

'There is a danger,' de Valera admitted, but he felt it could be minimised with the political advantage maximised if he could first get on the platform so that his arrest would be witnessed by the public.[83] This would not only demonstrate that the elections were not really free, but would also afford him a considerable amount of protection, as there could be no doubt that Free State authorities would be responsible if anything happened to him.

Taking great care to avoid detection, de Valera made his way to Ennis by a circuitous route. On the eve of his appearance he shaved off the beard and moustache he had been using for disguise, but he still managed to make it undetected to the platform in the square in Ennis. It was about 2.30 in the afternoon when he took off his coat and cap and walked to the front of the platform.

'There he is!' someone shouted. 'My God, 'tis himself.'[84]

A great roar went up. The Sinn Féin leader stood there looking unmoved. He seemed calm but looked pale and drawn. He then spoke a few perfunctory words in Irish before continuing in English:

> They spoke to you when we couldn't come to tell you the truth. They spoke to you and said that we were anarchists, and that we were out for destruction. We come here, and I come here as one to tell you that I have never stood for destruction. I have never stood for brother's hand being raised against brother's hand.
>
> I have never stood for playing the enemy's game in that one part of the Irish nation goes to fight the other part. I have always preached one and only one gospel, and that is the gospel I preach to you today, the one and only gospel, and that is that if the people of this country stood together and were united it could achieve complete independence.[85]

At that point an armoured car entered the square with two files of Free State troops, who surrounded the platform. Friends began to gather around de Valera. 'I have to go,' he shouted, 'but I am glad it is in Clare that I am being taken.'

Suddenly the soldiers began firing and elements of the crowd stampeded. Amid the confusion de Valera was knocked to the floor. One reporter noted that the Sinn Féin leader looked stunned and dazed as he lay on his face. When he finally sat up it was apparent that he had a leg injury. (Years later an X-ray detected a bullet fragment lodged in his leg muscle.)

On being approached by a Free State officer, de Valera made it clear that he was not resisting arrest and the soldiers should therefore have some consideration for the people. A number of those on the platform then tried to cling to de Valera as he limped off with the troops.

Throughout the civil war many of the Irregulars had looked on de Valera with suspicion; they did not agree with, or possibly understand his Document No. 2, and they were suspicious of his obvious lack of enthusiasm for the actual fighting, but with his arrest all that was forgotten. According to one editorial, he 'was captured just in time to escape oblivion.'[86] Whether that was true or not, there could be no doubt that his arrest propelled him back into the front line, as far as Republicans were concerned. He was again their real leader, and the vituperation of Free State authorities could only enhance his position among Republicans.

'We have arrested the man who called up anarchy and crime, and who did more damage than anyone could have conceived, or than was ever done by the British,' O'Higgins declared next day in Rathmines. 'Through him, and at his instigation, a number of young blackguards had robbed banks, blown up bridges, and wrecked railways, and that in the name of the Irish Republic.' O'Higgins added that 'the real issue in the election is — anarchy versus law and order, and the government candidates stand for law and order and decency.'[87]

No doubt O'Higgins personally believed what he was saying, but Republicans could hardly be blamed for seeing things differently. It was a strange kind of law and order that the Cumann na nGaedheal government was standing for when no one was ever brought to justice for the barbaric excesses of the Free State troops in Kerry. Nor were any charges brought against de Valera, who would have welcomed the chance to defend himself in court. He was convinced that he had acted honourably and correctly in both the period leading up to and during the civil war itself.

Cosgrave's cabinet decided that charges should be brought against de Valera 'with the least possible delay'. But the Attorney General quickly found that only a pathetic case could be mustered. In fact, the only documentary evidence he could find to substantiate any charge was an inflamatory letter de Valera had written to the secretary of Cumann na mBan on 5 January 1923. In view of the enormity of the accusations made by members of the government — most recently by O'Higgins in Rathmines — it would have led to a truly ludicrous situation had de Valera been charged only with inciting a women's organisation at the height of the civil war.[88] Yet instead of freeing him 'as a political curiosity',[89] like one American editorial suggested, the Minister of Defence, Richard Mulcahy, ordered that he should be held indefinitely on the grounds that he was a danger to public safety.

Meanwhile the election campaign continued. On the weekend following his arrest de Valera was supposed to appear at a public rally in Dublin. His eldest son, Vivion, who was still in short pants, took his place. 'My father promised that he would speak to you here today, Vivion began, 'and he is a man who would keep his word if he could. But he cannot speak to you today, for *giollai na nGall* (the servants of the foreigners) seized him in County Clare the other day and they have him in prison now. I know not what they will do with him.'[90] Young de Valera was then followed by the teenage son of the late Erskine Childers. The presence of the two boys provided a strong emotional appeal to people to support Republican candidates, especially as the ruling Cumann na nGaedheal was acting with what Alfred Blanche, the French Consul-General, described as 'the same odious high-handedness' that had characterised all its actions since coming to power.[91] In fact, Blanche, who had been in Dublin since 1917, observed that the former British regime was heavenly in comparison to the Cosgrave Government. Perhaps this explained the surprisingly good showing made by the Republicans at the polls.

Sinn Féin candidates ran unexpectedly well in gaining over 27 per cent of the votes and winning 44 seats, which was more than any of them had anticipated. Although Cumann na nGaedheal, which won 63 of the 153 seats, was denied a majority, it was still easily able to form a government, because the Sinn Féin deputies had no intention of taking their seats.

CHAPTER SIX

# Regaining the Citadel

*From Prison to the Presidency*

For more than six of the eleven months of his imprisonment de Valera was held in solitary confinement. If Free State authorities were hoping to force him to agree to some kind of formal peace, they were sadly mistaken because he was not about to do so, either implicitly or otherwise. He believed it would yet be possible to achieve his objectives by democratic means.

As one point he managed to get a letter to his designated successor, Paddy Ruttledge, advising Republicans on the outside to stand for fair play and justice by advocating programmes which would be advantageous to all classes. 'The more we lean to the economic side,' de Valera wrote, 'the better it will be for the political objective but it must be a national programme for the common good, not a class programme.'[1]

Republican prisoners were gradually released, with de Valera eventually being freed in July 1924. One of his first tasks was to do something about the Emergency Government set up during the Civil War. Although he had been leaning towards abandoning that arrangement before his arrest, he either had a change of heart in the interim, or else realised that the scheme had become so important as a symbol to Republicans in his absence that he could not just forget about it.

There were, however, some real difficulties in trying to preserve even the nominal existence of the Emergency Government, which had supposedly been set up by 'the faithful members' of the second Dáil. A number of Republican deputies, who had not been members of the latter, had since been elected in June 1922 or August 1923, but they had no legal standing within the Emergency set-up, as the second Dáil was still supposedly the *de jure* parliament.

Faced with the difficulty of finding a proper role for the new deputies, de Valera decided to establish *Comhairle na dTeachtaí* in which members of the second Dáil would sit together with those who had been elected subsequently. At the first meeting of the new body on 7 August 1924 he explained that his cabinet colleagues were unanimous that the Emergency Government* should be maintained. 'There was not the slightest doubt in any of our minds,' he said, 'that the proper course was to keep the government in existence. It will be there to take over the government of the country at anytime when the people will make it impossible for the other crowd to carry on as a government.' He proposed replacing the Council of State with *Comhairle na dTeachtaí*, which the second Dáil could then authorise to function as 'the actual government of the country'. In short, the second Dáil would be the *de jure* government, while *Comhairle na dTeachtaí* would, in theory, be the *de facto* one. Of course, de Valera privately accepted that the Free State Dáil was really the *de facto* government of the country. Thus, in the eyes of Republicans, *Comhairle na dTeachtaí* would be the *de jure de facto* government, while the parliament in Leinster House would be the actual *de facto* government.[2]

The complexities of the situation in which the Republicans were involving themselves were such that one can only wonder if anybody present really understood what de Valera meant when he summarised their difficulties by concluding:

> The material point is whether the second Dáil should meet now and hand over its powers and authorities to the body that was subsequently elected, and whether they should meet afterwards and hand over to the body recently elected the powers they subsequently had.[3]

On being questioned, de Valera explained that he did not envision the Emergency Government operating as a rival to that of the Free State but 'simply a preparatory

* Though the term 'government' normally refers to the parliamentary executive, in the case of the Emergency Government it was used interchangeably to cover both the executive and the legislature.

government, getting ready to take over the work of the government. 'In essence it would operate in much the same way as an opposition party with a shadow cabinet, except that it would sit separately and maintain that it was the *de jure* government. It could, he said, 'be regarded as the proper authority to be obeyed by the mass of the citizens if they were willing to obey it.'[4]

Believing that the people would eventually realise that he had been right about the Treaty, de Valera was confident that the country would sooner or later turn to the Republicans, and he argued that it would be advantageous if they could then form a government which could trace its origins directly from the Dáil of the 1919-1922 period. In the course of his remarks he made one very perceptive observation about the partition provisions of the Treaty. 'The clause about the Boundary Commission was a ridiculous clause,' he said. 'It was meant to fool and could be used at any time to get out of anything on the grounds that the taking away of portion of the Six Counties might be uneconomical.' This was exactly what did happen late the following year.[5]

In the interim de Valera continued to put increasing public emphasis on his dissatisfaction with the partition question, as when he went back to Ennis on 15 August 1924 for an address on the spot where he had been arrested exactly a year earlier.

Observing that a number of reporters were present in the hope he might announce some new policy, he emphasised he was still pursuing the same aims as he was in 1917 and thereafter. Those aims, he said, precluded 'very definitely' first of all any possible assent by us to the dismemberment of our country. You cannot have a sovereign Ireland if you have an Ireland cut in two.' He went on to defend himself against the charge of being undemocratic. 'Let no one,' he said, 'taunt us with being undemocratic. We realise the difficulties of uniting in the cause of freedom. We know that in such a fight there has to be a vanguard, and we know that very often it is only a few choice spirits can form that vanguard.' He urged the gathering to pursue Republican aims without deviation. 'If you keep the straight road, he concluded, 'no matter how difficult it may be, every inch you go is an inch of progress.'[6]

In Dundalk the following week, he explained that he had refused to take his seat at Leinster House because it was a partition parliament.[7] This was obviously a disingenuous explanation, seeing that he was already on record in a letter to Mary MacSwiney stating that if the oath were removed, the question of entering the Free State Dáil 'would be a matter purely of tactics and expediency.'[8] Nevertheless he acted publicly as if he was abstaining on the principle that taking his seat would amount to formal recognition of partition.

When elections were called in Northern Ireland in the autumn of 1924 de Valera announced that Sinn Féin would put forward candidates so that the people in the area could demonstrate 'their detestation' of partition by voting for those who would 'deny the right of England to make partition laws, or any other laws, for this country, and who will pledge themselves accordingly not to sit in the parliament of England.'[9] He went so far as defending the seat he had won himself in south Down in May 1921. When he went to speak in Newry, he was arrested, served with an exclusion order, and put back over the border. The following day he ignored the order and crossed the border again — this time to speak in Derry, but he was arrested outside the hall and taken to Belfast, where he refused to recognise the court.

'I decline to plead before this court,' he told the magistrate, 'because I don't recognise that this court has authority, seeing it is the creature of a foreign power and is therefore not sanctioned by the Irish people.' That was the extent of his defence. 'I have nothing further to say,' he explained on being threatened with contempt of court, 'except that I don't recognise the court.' The magistrate then found him guilty of violating the exclusion order and sentenced him to a month in Crumlin Road Jail.'[10]

The publicity generated by his actions helped create the mistaken impression that the partition issue had been a major consideration in his opposition to the Treaty. Indeed this impression would eventually become quite widespread. Yet, although he had accepted the Boundary Commission idea in December 1921, he did become critical of the scheme long before the Boundary Commission began its deliberations, with the result that he benefited politically from the backlash that followed the ensuing debacle.

People in the Free State had been led to believe that the Boundary Commission was going to carve off large areas of the Six Counties. Collins had publicly stated on a number of occasions that so much territory would be given to the Free State that Northern Ireland would become an unviable economic entity and would therefore be forced to unite with the rest of the island. Consequently there was amazement in late November 1925 when the *Morning Post* revealed that the draft terms of the commission's report envisaged a two-way transfer of territory with parts of Counties Donegal and Monahan being given to Northern Ireland, which would lose about the same amount of territory elsewhere. The Commission had ironically concurred with Collins's assessment that the transfer of nationalist areas would render Northern Ireland an unviable economic entity, but it went on to conclude — as de Valera had privately predicted — that this would violate the provision in the Treaty stipulating that the transfer of territory should be made in accordance with economic and geographical considerations. Since Lloyd George had already explained publicly that the stipulation in question had been included in the Treaty simply to prevent the transfer of isolated areas such as Unionist areas of Dublin or Nationalist areas of Belfast, there could be little doubt that the Boundary Commission's findings were a violation of the spirit of the Treaty, but the Free State had been so weakened by the civil war that it was not in a position to resist forcefully.

The Free State's representative resigned from the Commission and a delegation from Dublin hastily tried to rectify the situation by concluding an agreement in which the commission's findings were set aside. The Free State dropped its claim to territory and, in return, the British released the Dublin government from its obligations under the Treaty to assume a portion 'of the Public Debt of the United Kingdom'.

De Valera denounced the settlement. He contended that

no section of the country was 'entitled to secede from this nation, and secession ought not to be tolerated and, if it can be prevented, ought to be prevented, and on no account whatever should the national consent be given to it.' The Sinn Féin leader was particularly critical of the fact that nationalist areas — especially those adjacent to the border — were being abandoned to Orange domination. 'To my mind,' he said, 'to abandon these communities for any consideraton whatever is not merely an act of unpardonable injustice but a national disgrace.' He certainly did not think the financial gains made in London compensated for the loss of territory which should rightfully have been given to the Free State. 'Let no Irishman think,' he declared, 'that we have gained anything more than avoiding the possibility of being cheated further.'[11]

Strong pressure was exerted on de Valera and his colleagues to enter Leinster House. Opposition leaders in the Dáil invited them to a meeting in the Shelbourne Hotel, Dublin, on 8 December 1925 in an effort to persuade them to take their seats in order to defeat the boundary agreement. Afterwards the Sinn Féin deputies, who had been encouraged to go to the Shelbourne by de Valera, met separately. Some of them tried to persuade their colleagues to go into the Dáil to defeat the agreement and then withdraw again, but there were doubts whether they would be able to muster enough support to be successful.

De Valera vacillated, but then he had to move cautiously because there were already signs of a developing split within Republican ranks. Only the previous month a General Convention of the Republcan Army passed a resolution severing the organisation's connection with the Emergency Government after Frank Aiken admitted that Sinn Féin was considering entering Leinster house. Not only was de Valera's leadership effectively challenged by the army's withdrawl of the nominal allegiance it had given to the Emergency Government in October 1922, but he was also confronted with a further challenge at the Sinn Féin Árd Fheis four days later when a resolution was introduced calling for the formal abandonment of Document No. 2 'as a basis for any future treaty' because, it was contended, that the alternative 'would not now be an equitable settlement between this nation and England.'[12] Arguing that External Association would be necessary to attract the Unionists of Northern Ireland into a united Ireland, de Valera managed to get the motion withdrawn before it came to a vote, but he must still have been mindful of the delicate position of his own leadership three weeks later when the question of entering the Dáil came to the fore.

'Much as I loved Dev,' Gerry Boland recalled years later, 'there were times when he could not just make up his mind.'[13] This was one such occasion. De Valera eventually went along with the decision of a majority of Sinn Féin representatives not to enter Leinster House. They decided instead to make their own rather futile gesture of holding a public meeting at the Rotunda, where the Irish Volunteers had been founded to counter the threat of partition in 1913. Thus, while the controversial agreement was going through its second reading at Leinster House, Sinn Féin deputies could only make a rather pathetic denunciation of partition at a public meeting. (The Cosgrave government actually had sufficient support to ensure ratification of the agreement, even if Sinn Féin deputies had taken their seats and voted against it.)

Within a matter of days de Valera began taking steps towards revising the abstentionist policy. On 18 December 1925 he suggested at a meeting of *Comhairle na dTeachtaí* that the policy should be reviewed. Two weeks later he announced publicly that he would personally be prepared to enter the Dáil, if he could do so without having to take the oath. On 12 January 1926 he persuaded the Sinn Féin Executive to call an extraordinary Árd Fheis on 9 March 1926 to consider the whole question, but he did not advocate 'immediate entry' into Leinster House. In fact, he publicly emphasised that no Republican could enter as long as the taking of the oath was a prerequisite. 'The oath of allegiance to a foreign power,' he declared, 'is now, as it has always been, a barrier which no one may cross and remain a representative, or even a member of, the Sinn Féin organisation.'[14]

The need for a viable alternative to the Cosgrave government was important in view of what many people considered the government's ineptitude in handling Anglo-Irish relations. Indeed it would later become apparent that there was another instance of ineffectiveness in March 1926 with the finalisation of the so-called Ultimate Financial Settlement in which the Free State acknowledged, in effect, that it would continue to make annuity payments to Britain for lands purchased under the terms of the various land acts passed around the turn of the century, although the wording of the agreement doing away with the Boundary Commission seemed to absolve the Free State from such payments.

Thus the Boundary Commission agreement together with the Ultimate Financial settlement really confirmed some of de Valera's worst predictions. The time was certainly ripe for him to enter the Dáil, but he was confronted with real difficulties in persuading some of his Sinn Féin colleagues to go along with him. Prior to his arrest in 1923 he made it clear to Mary MacSwiney that the obligation to take the oath was the only matter of principle on which he was in favour of abstaining from the Dáil, but while he was in jail she managed to persuade the party to adopt a more radical policy of refusing to recognise the Free State government, its legislature, or institutions, so that by the time of his release her policy had taken a firm root. When he tried 'to bring the policy back to the point it should never have changed from,' he ran into opposition from those who looked on his approach as 'a complete change of front.'[15] They were unwilling to abandon abstentionism, even if the oath were abolished.

When the Árd Fheis met on 9 March 1926 de Valera proposed:

> That once the admission of oaths of the Twenty-six County and Six County Assemblies are removed, it becomes a question not of principle but of policy, whether or not Republican representatives should attend these Assemblies.

After some objections were raised he accepted the following addendum:

> Provided that no recognition as a sovereign body be

accorded to either institution, and that the continuity of Dáil Éireann [i.e. the second Dáil] as the *de jure* Government of all Ireland continues to be maintained.[16]

But this did not satisfy diehards like Father Michael O'Flanagan, the longtime Vice-President of Sinn Féin. He introduced an amendment to prohibit representatives of the party from entering 'into any usurping legislature set up by English law in Ireland.' The amendment was passed narrowly by 223 to 218, but when the full amended resolution was then moved, it was defeated by 179 to 177 with 85 abstentions. As a result matters were really left where they had been before the Árd Fheis, which was undoubtedly a defeat for de Valera. He therefore resigned as President of Sinn Féin on 11 March 1926.

Although de Valera had indicated by accepting the addendum that he was not foresaking the *de jure* position claimed for the Emergency Government, there was rumour that he no longer intended to maintain that position when *Comhairle na dTeachtaí* convened a fortnight later. According to Mary MacSwiney this 'rumour proved true to an extent that I would not have believed possible. In the course of the meeting it was clear that the mentality of Dev and his party had changed considerably, and they were no longer willing to contemplate our holding the Government position, and letting them carry on without any risk of compromising that position.' She wrote that de Valera and his supporters wanted:

1. To relegate Dáil Éireann [i.e. the second Dáil] to a mythical region where it might get some formal recognition, but with a clear understanding that it should claim no rights, nor try to exercise any.
2. That the person elected should be President of *Comhairle na dTeachtaí* not President of the Republic since January 1922.[17]

The debate became quite acrimonious, and was, in fact, reminiscent of the bitterness of the Treaty debate. 'It was horrible,' MacSwiney wrote. At one point de Valera said that he would proposed one of the hardliners, Art

O'Connor, as chief executive of *Comhairle na dTeachtaí*, if the latter would form a coalition executive. The hardliners agreed provided that de Valera and his supporters were prepared not only to continue recognising the Emergency Government as *de jure*, and to refuse to take the Treaty-oath, but also to promise in the event of securing a majority at a general election, they would ignore the Free State Constitution, frame a new one, and summon an all-Ireland parliament in which representatives from the Six Counties would be permitted to sit. What they were advocating, in essence, was that de Valera and the others could go ahead with their plans, and if they succeeded, then the second Dáil could be dissolved. If they failed, on the other hand, she felt that the hardliners 'would still be holding the fort, and we could go forward on the same platform.'[18]

De Valera and his supporters nevertheless rejected those conditions for a coalition. 'Honestly,' MacSwiney wrote to Seán T. O'Kelly in the United States, 'I cannot see why that should have annoyed them. It was exactly the point of view expressed by Dev himself a few months before.' If he had the support of a majority, she thought he would have welcomed strong opposition, but he resented it when he was in a minority. 'Anyhow, be that as it may,' MacSwiney continued, 'the other side took the same poor attitude to my poor self as the Treaty people did a few years ago. Even Dev was as nasty as he could be. He has given me some surprises in these past months I can tell you.' She felt that she and her colleagues were following the same line adopted in 1922, while he now seemed ready to adopt the very policy of 'accepting the Treaty position but not the Treaty,' which was what those whom she called 'the Traitors' had advocated four years earlier. 'If he is taking risks as he says,' she continued, 'he may call and think us who will not take those risks "cowards" if he likes, but one does not like to see him doing the very thing he was the first to blame others for — try to pull down and belittle the very thing he helped to build.'[19]

In order to bring matters to a head, a resolution was proposed to the effect that *Comhairle na dTeachtaí* did 'not approve of the policy as outlined by the President.'[20] This virtual censure motion was carried by 19 votes to 18, and de Valera then resigned as President of the Emergency Government and was promptly replaced by Art O'Connor.

A couple of weeks later de Valera announced the formation of a new party called 'Fianna Fáil (Republican Party)'* whose aims he outlined as securing the political independence of the whole island as a republic, restoring the Irish language, developing a social system affording equal opportunities 'to every Irish citizen to live a noble and useful Christian life', redistributing land in order 'to get the greatest number of Irish families possible rooted in the soil', and making Ireland as economically self-contained and self-sufficient as possible.[21]

Fianna Fáil was formally launched at La Scala Theatre in Dublin on 26 May 1926 with de Valera being elected President of the party. He explained at the time that Fianna Fáil's immediate aim was to remove the oath, and once this had been done it would be possible to advance the national cause by 'cutting the bonds of foreign interference one by one until the full internal sovereignty of the Twenty-six Counties was established beyond question.'[22]

'With a united Twenty-six Counties,' he added, 'the position would be reached in which the solution of the problem of successfully bringing in the North could be confidently undertaken.' Of course, entering the Free State Dáil entailed recognising the existence of partition, but he contended that this did not mean they would be endorsing it. 'To recognise the existence of facts, as we must, is not to acquiesce in them,' he declared. 'We have been in no way a party to the partition of our country. . . We have not accepted it and do not accept it. We shall at all times be morally free to use any means that God gives us to reunite the country and win back the part of our Ulster province that has been taken away from us.'

De Valera travelled throughout the country helping to organise Fianna Fáil at local levels. His message, in effect, was that although Republicans had previously contended that the Emergency Government was *de jure* and that the

* The actual translation of Fianna Fáil is 'Soldiers of Destiny', but Republican Party was placed in brackets after the name at the insistence of Seán Lemass.

Irish Republic was still in existence, it was now necessary to face realities. 'If we do not recognise the facts,' he declared in Ennis on 29 June 1926, 'we cannot make progress. For the moment we have been driven out of the citadel and I am asking our people to attack it again and retake it. I cannot rally the people to a fresh attack if I keep shouting that I have got the citadel already.'

Although he tried to play down the significance of his break with Sinn Féin, Mary MacSwiney publicly accused him of moving dangerously close to the stand he had refused to take when invited by Collins back in 1922. 'The policy now adopted by Fianna Fáil,' she asserted in a letter to the press, 'seems to be just that which we refused four years ago — "accepting the Treaty position, but not accepting the Treaty". If that was not a proper policy for Republicans in 1922, how can it be right in 1926?'[23]

De Valera formally recognised the Free State's authority and its British connection later that year by applying for a Free State passport in order to go to the United States, where he hoped to embarrass the Cosgrave government by frustrating its efforts to get hold of $2,500,000 that he had deposited in the name of the Irish Republic in 1920. He had earlier suggested that the money be used for some non-political purpose like having an independent body set up to preserve the Irish language, but that suggestion was contemptuously dismissed by a member of the Cosgrave government, who said that the Gaelic League would get all the money it wanted in Ireland. De Valera realised that there was little chance of regaining control of the money himself, but he felt that it would be a worthwhile propaganda exercise if he could get the American courts to rule that the Free State was not the legitimate successor of the first or second Dáil.

'These funds,' de Valera contended upon his arrival in New York on 5 March 1927, 'can be legitimately disbursed only for the purposes of an all-Ireland Government functioning independently without any acceptance of British interference or control.'[24]

In addition to testifying in the court case, he also toured the United States raising funds for Fianna Fáil which, he explained, needed to win the support of the majority of the Irish people at the polls before it would be possible to achieve Republican goals. 'We can rally and reorganise the Irish people,' he told an overflow crowd at Carnegie Hall, 'but we cannot obtain the support of world opinion against England, our real enemy, until a majority of the people's representatives are with us.'[25]

De Valera's speeches tended to exploit the anglophobia of his Irish-American audience. 'Some of those listening to me,' he told a gathering in St Paul, Minnesota, for instance, 'believe, no doubt, the story that the British army have evacuated Ireland. When I left Cobh on this trip I passed out between the forts which guard Cork Harbour. By whom were these forts manned? By Irish troops? By Free State troops even? Not at all. They are held by British troops and the British flag flies over them.'[26] While speaking in Boston he contended that Britain's retention of Irish bases had implications even in the United States.

'The United States has been the best friend of Ireland,' he said, 'yet if England should go to war with this country we would be obliged to submit to seeing our land used as a base to fight our best friend.' He added that Ireland could not be considered free while her territory could be used in this way. 'We only ask,' de Valera added, 'that our people be permitted to choose, without hinderance and interference, the form of government they desire.'[27]

Such remarks went some way towards repairing the enormous damage he had done to his own standing in 1922, and he was further helped by the New York Supreme Court, which ruled that the disputed money should be returned to subscribers on the grounds that the Republican Government of 1919-1922 had never been officially recognised, with the result that the Free State could not therefore succeed it. The ruling was widely seen as a triumph for the Fianna Fáil leader, who had secured what amounted to an eminent independent judgment that the Irish Free State was not the legitimate successor of the Irish Republic, notwithstanding the result of the general election of June 1922.

Thus de Valera's American visit provided both a propaganda victory and some much needed funds for Fianna

Fáil, but his reception in America bore little resemblance to that he had received during his earlier visit. Although his authorised biographers made much of his welcome in Boston, where some 5,000 peple came out to hear him speak just before his return home, this crowd really paled into insignificance when compared to the 50,000 that thronged into Fenway Park to see him in June 1919.

Shortly after returning home, de Valera had a chance to test his new party's strength at the polls when Cosgrave called a general election for June 1927. Fianna Fáil made a very impressive showing in its first outing, winning 44 seats, just three short of the ruling Cumann na nGaedheal, which lost heavily at the hands of small parties. Without the abstentionists in Fianna Fáil and Sinn Féin taking their seats, Cumann na nGaedheal still did not have a majority in the Dáil.

On 23 June 1927 de Valera and his Fianna Fáil colleagues tried to claim their seats, but they were stopped and told that they would first have to subscribe their names to a book containing the Treaty-oath. This, they refused to do. Afterwards they issued a statement to the effect that 'under no circumstances whatever' would they subscribe to that oath. They planned instead to force a referendum in order to abolish the oath under the provisions of an article of the Free State constitution which stipulated that the parliament would have to submit any constitutional amendment to a referendum of the people on being petitioned to do so by at least 75,000 eligible voters. As rounding up that many names posed little problem, there was a real chance that Fianna Fáil would be able to use constitutional means to get rid of the oath.

Speaking in Ennis on 10 July 1927 de Valera contended that the Treaty, which specified that 'the oath to be taken by members of the parliament of the Irish Free State' would be as prescribed, had not made the oath obligatory. It had not actually stipulated that an oath had to be taken. In other words, no oath was necessary, but if there was one, it would be as prescribed in the Treaty. He argued that the Cosgrave government was deliberately retaining the oath as a political means of ensuring that conscientious Republicans would not enter the Dáil.

In ancient times, de Valera added, the walls of Bandon bore the inscription: 'Beggar, Jew, atheist may enter here, but not a Papist'. Now, he said, the authorities of the Free State were inscribing their own slogan over government buildings: 'Unionist, Orangeman, anarchist may enter here, but not a Republican'.[28] Such a charge certainly had an emotional appeal but the whole political climate was wrecked elsewhere the same day with the assassination of Vice-President Kevin O'Higgins in Dublin.

De Valera roundly denounced the killing. 'The assassination of Mr O'Higgins is murder, and is inexcusable from any standpoint.' he declared. 'It is a crime that cuts at the root of representative government, and no one who realises what the crime means can do otherwise than deplore and condemn it. Every right-minded individual will deeply sympathise with the bereaved widow in her agony.'[29]

Following the assassination the Cosgrave government exploited popular indignation to rush through legislation forcing Fianna Fáil deputies to swallow their pride and take the oath, or face extinction as a political party. The legislation not only did away with the right to call a constitutional referendum by public petition, but also stipulated that henceforth all Dáil candidates would have to sign an affidavit that they would take their seats within two months, if elected. Any candidate refusing to comply would be disqualified.

De Valera publicly reaffirmed his determination not to take the oath on 24 July 1927, but quickly made it clear that if Thomas Johnson, the leader of the Labour Party, managed to form a coalition government and then did away with the oath so that Fianna Fáil deputies could take their seats without having to subscribe to that obnoxious test, they would promise not to 'press any issues involving the Treaty to the point of overthrowing such a government during the normal lifetime of the present assembly.'[30] Yet the Labour Party really had little chance of forming a government without the active help of Fianna Fáil.

Behind the scenes, however, de Valera was wavering.

He later explained that he came to the conclusion that 'short of a miracle, or a successful armed conflict', there was no way of achieving Republican goals if he and his colleagues continued to abstain from the Dáil.[31] He therefore seized a way out provided by members of Cumann na nGaedheal who had consistently maintained, ever since the signing of the Treaty, that the oath was just a formality with no binding significance.

'I asked myself,' de Valera explained, 'whether in a crisis like that I would be justified in staying outside if it were, in fact, true that this thing was a mere formality.'[32] As a result he began seriously considering what he previously had depicted as unthinkable — the possibility of subscribing to the oath in order to enter the Dáil.

Johnson was approached as to what he would do in return, if Fianna Fáil deputies backed him to replace Cosgrave as President of the Executive Council. In reply, he promised that if elected, he would 'make every effort to get the oath removed or altered "by *agreement* with the British government", and if he found it impossible to do so "within a reasonable time", he would resign.'[33] This was enough to interest Fianna Fáil leaders who then set out their own conditions.

On 9 August 1927 Johnson agreed to the most important of the conditions. If elected, he promised that he would take immediate steps to have a constitutional referendum held on the question of abolishing the oath. Next day Fianna Fáil formally decided to subscribe to the book containing the oath, but they first issued a statement emphasising that they were merely subscribing to what had been characterised as an empty political formula. The statement, which was signed by forty-two deputies, emphasised that they proposed 'to regard the declaration as an empty formality and repeat that their only allegiance is to the Irish nation and that it will be given to no other power or authority.'[34]

On entering Leinster House, de Valera presented the clerk with a copy of the signed statement. 'I am not prepared to take an oath,' he declared in Irish. 'I am not going to take an oath. I am prepared to put my name down in this book in order to get permission to go into the Dáil, but it has no other significance.'

De Valera then picked up a Bible that was on the table and moved it to the other side of the room. 'You must remember,' he stressed upon returning, 'that I am taking no oath.' Then placing some paper over the writing at the top of the page, he signed his name.[35]

'I signed it in the same way as I would sign an autograph in a newspaper,' he explained afterwards. 'If you ask me whether I had an idea what was there, I say "yes".' But, he emphasised, 'it was neither read to me, nor was I asked to read it.'[36]

The first Dáil vote that de Valera and his colleagues participated in was a momentous one. The Labour Party had tabled a motion of no confidence in the government. Not only was Johnson confident of winning, but Cosgrave had already resigned himself to defeat. In the ensuing debate Fianna Fáil deputies kept a low profile. In fact, the only one of them to speak was Seán T. O'Kelly, who said just a few words in Irish to explain that there was no need to say any more as everybody in the assembly knew where his party stood on the issue. Shortly before the vote one of those who was supposed to support the motion left the Dáil, with the result that there was a tie, which the Speaker broke by using his casting vote to kill the motion.

Had the motion carried, Johnson would undoubtedly have been able to form a coalition government because in accordance with established practice the Dáil would have had to vote for its own dissolution, so there would have been little chance of Cosgrave being able to call a general election. After the vote the Dáil adjourned for the remainder of the summer, and it was during the recess that the President took the unprecedented step of asking the Governor-General to dissolve the assembly and call another election.

This time Cumann na nGaedheal gained twenty-one seats, so that with the help of the Farmers' Party, it was able to form a stable government. Nevertheless Fianna Fáil consolidated its own position as the second largest party in the Dáil by increasing its representation by thirteen seats.

As leader of the opposition during the next four and a half years de Valera used every opportunity to appeal to the nationalistic instincts of the Irish people, especially when he was able to offset his own position against what he believed was a weak, subservient approach pursued by the Cosgrave government in its relations with Britain. He thereby managed to exploit skilfully the anti-British sentiment that was still rife in the country.

When the government announced that it had been invited by the United States to sign the Kellog-Briande Pact, a treaty which sought to outlaw war, de Valera used the occasion to express reservations about the pact by linking it both with the partition question and his earlier opposition to Article X of the Covenant of the League of Nations. It was not that he was in favour of war. 'I have no doubt whatever,' he said, 'that the people of this country would be anxious to see a genuine treaty arrived at between the nations by which war would be outlawed.' Just as he had complained about Article X in 1919, he now criticised the pact on the grounds that Britain would be able to use it to hold people in subjugation by insisting that pact signatories desist from actively supporting struggles of national liberation within the British Empire. 'As far as we on this side of the House are concerned,' de Valera stressed, 'we want to be disassociated from any form of reply that would imply that we recognise Great Britain's right either to hold this country or any other country.'[37] He was, of course, emphasising by implication the right of the Irish people to resort to force in order to bring about Irish unity.

De Valera deftly managed to create the impression that there was a real difference between his attitude towards partition and that of the Cumann na nGaedheal government. Authorities in Northern Ireland certainly helped boost that impression by arresting him again for ignoring the exclusion order when he crossed the border to open a bazaar in Belfast in February 1929. He then enlisted further nationalist sympathy by insisting on speaking Irish in court, which drew the ire of the judge, who sentenced him to another month in jail.

Probably the item of most substance on which Fianna

Fáil managed to show up the government concerned the payment to Britain of land annuities. De Valera contended that they should be withheld because the Dublin government had no obligation to pay them. He had a very good case.

The Partition Act of 1920 had specified that the land annuities would be handed over to the respective parliaments in Dublin and Belfast. In explaining the legislation at the time Lloyd George had declared that the annuities were being 'handed to the Irish governments as a free gift for the purpose of the development and improvement of Ireland.' Admittedly, Article 5 of the Treaty subsequently acknowledged that the Free State would 'assume liability for the service of the public debt of the United Kingdom' but it added that 'any just claims on the part of Ireland' would be taken into account. The Irish signatories had not admitted a responsibility to pay any money; they had only agreed that the question should be considered at a later date and that the Free State would pay, if it could be shown that she owed anything. Collins, who did the bulk of the negotiating on financial issues, had argued that the British actually owed money to Ireland as a result of over-taxation during the nineteenth century. Consequently, as far as de Valera was concerned, the Cosgrave government had made a disastrous blunder in handing over the land annuities, but that was only part of the Fianna Fáil leader's case. Article 2 of the Boundary Commission agreement of 1925 had stipulated that the Free State was being 'released from the obligation under Article 5' of the Treaty, so if the land annuities had been owed prior to 1925, they were not thereafter, notwithstanding the blunder by Cosgrave's Minister of Finance in apparently agreeing to pay the annuities as part of the Ultimate Financial Settlement of 1926. De Valera refused to accept the latter agreement as binding because it had never been submitted to the Dáil for ratification. As a result, he contended that it was not worth the paper on which it was written. 'No minister can assign national property away by his own signature,' he declared. 'This has never got statutory sanction, and every sum paid out in virtue of that agreement without collateral statutory sanction is being paid out without the proper authority.'[38]

De Valera also pressed again for the removal of the oath by contending that the Treaty had not made it obligatory. This argument no doubt had a certain vicarious appeal for many people in the Twenty-six Counties, who felt justifiably aggrieved that the Boundary Commission's rigid interpretation of the Treaty had robbed the Free State of the contiguous Nationalist areas of Northern Ireland.

In his quest to further the cause of full national independence de Valera believed that Fianna Fáil was being seriously hampered by its inability to get its message across properly to the people because of the hostility of the press. He therefore decided to establish a daily newspaper himself, and he made two separate fund-raising visits to the United States. 'There is nothing so important for Ireland as a newspaper that will champion her freedom,' he told the press upon his arrival in New York on 10 December 1929. Although his fund-raising activities were curtailed by the death of his step-father the following week in Rochester, New York, he nevertheless managed to raise $80,000 during the six and a half weeks he was in America. He returned again the following December, and this time spent almost six months touring the United States raising funds.

'The harm that is being done to our country through the lack of an independent, constructive and critical national journal is incalculable,' he declared upon his arrival in New York. 'They make no national appeal whatever. The result is that the circulation in Ireland of British newspapers such as the *Daily Mail,* the *Daily Express,* and *Daily Chronicle* has been rapidly increasing. The whole thought and philosophy behind these newspapers is entirely alien. Everyone who is interested in preserving our national individuality is alarmed at the prospect of a further increase in their circulation, and it is realised that the only effective remedy is to provide an alternative — produce an Irish paper which the Irish people will spontaneously support because it stands for Ireland and Irish interests, and is representative of their own thoughts and ideals.'[39] This appeal to save the Irish people from the pernicious British press undoubtedly had a particularly strong appeal to anglophobic Irish-Americans.

De Valera also stressed other anti-British themes during his travels, such as repeating his contention that Ireland would be bound by the Treaty to help Britain in an Anglo-American war, or criticising Britain for extracting what he depicted as exorbitantly high land annuity payments, which he compared to the comparatively modest war debt payments that Britain was making to the United States. He pointed out that in proportion to its population, Ireland was paying Britain sixty-six times more annually than Britain was paying to the United States.[40]

While this tour, like his two previous ones, lacked the enthusiasm of de Valera's first visit in 1919, it was nevertheless a financial success — especially as the United States was already in the throes of the Great Depression. The Fianna Fáil leader returned home in late May 1930 with sufficient funds to launch the *Irish Press* in September of the following year.

Meanwhile the Cosgrave government had been pursuing a policy that was designed to demonstrate that the Free State was as free as the dominions and was, in effect, independent. In view of Collins' contention that the Treaty provided the 'freedom to achieve freedom' the government felt the psychological need to provide visible manifestations of the country's independence, which was done in a number of ways. The Free State joined the League of Nations and registered the 1921 Treaty at Geneva, thereby securing what amounted to formal international recognition of the country as a separate national entity. This was further demonstrated with the appointment of a minister to Washington and the opening of formal diplomatic relations with the United States in 1924, although authorities in Dublin played down the fact that the Irish Minister was officially designated as His Majesty's Plenipotentiary.[41] Further Ministers were also appointed to the Vatican, France and Germany, in addition to having a permanent representative at the League of Nations in Geneva.

Membership of the League offered several ways of securing additional recognition of the country's independence by allowing Irish authorities to express unsolicited opinions on world issues, to take independent stands in voting, and to seek leadership roles within the organisation. Desmond FitzGerald, who served for a time as Cosgrave's Minister of External Affairs, admitted that 'every matter that came up' in the League was viewed 'from the aspect of narrow nationalism'.[42] In 1926 the Free State sought a seat on the Council of the organisation. Although that hastily prepared effort won little support, a similar effort was successful four years later.

From the standpoint of obtaining recognition of the country's independence, the most significant development was the enactment of the Statute of Westminister in 1931, which made the *de facto* status of the dominions *de jure*. This proved de Valera wrong, as he had contended during the Treaty debate that Britain would not accord the *de facto* status to the Free State. Some British politicians, most prominent among whom was Winston Churchill, did indeed try to have the Free State specifically excluded from the Statute of Westminster on the grounds that the country did not enjoy the real status of a dominion, as. Britain retained Irish bases and enjoyed defence concessions provided by none of the other dominions. No doubt the realisation that de Valera would again benefit politically weighed heavily on the British, because Churchill's arguments were ignored when Cosgrave insisted that the Treaty specifically guaranteed the Free State's status would be no less than that of Canada or the other dominions. Thus, when the Statute of Westminster became law in December 1931, the Irish Free State was recognised as master of her own destiny, enjoying equal rights with Britain and the other dominions in matters of internal policy.

In January 1932 the Dáil was dissolved and a general election called for the following month. The Cosgrave government tried to campaign on its record, particularly the role it had played in securing the Statute of Westminster, but the electorate were obviously more interested in other questions, especially economic problems, as the country was in the midst of the economic depression and the government seemed to be following austere financial policies with an almost masochistic zeal.

Although Fianna Fáil stressed the need for alternative economic policies, such as land distribution and the introduction of tariffs to protect and foster native industry in order to alleviate the chronic unemployment situation, de Valera cited the abolition of the oath as his primary goal. He also stressed that Fianna Fáil would suspend payments to Britain of the land annuities, which he equated with the reparation payments imposed on Germany following the Great War. At the time those reparations were popularly believed to be so heavy that they had undermined the world economy. Yet de Valera noted that the Free State was paying comparatively more to Britain annually, than Germany was being asked to pay. He added the emotive charge that the country was actually paying Britain for damage that had been done by the Black and Tans.

In the emotional atmosphere of the campaign it was not long before there were charges that de Valera was a communist or that at best he was a weak Kerensky who would be toppled by communists in Fianna Fáil once the party came to power. Even Cosgrave stooped to insinuations, such as telling a public gathering in Tralee that his party was 'against Communism and Russianism'.[43] There could be no mistaking the snide implication that Fianna Fáil was not opposed to those things.

The following week de Valera issued an election manifesto on behalf of Fianna Fáil promising, if elected with a majority, not to exceed its requested mandate 'without again consulting the people'. The manifesto went on to stress that the party had 'no leaning towards communism and no belief in communistic doctrines'.[44]

'I am not a communist,' de Valera declared on campaigning in Tralee next day. 'I am quite the reverse.' He stressed that Fianna Fáil aimed at creating a greater number of individual land owners by distributing land and increasing the number of homesteads on it. His opponents, he continued, were creating a red scare only to bolster their own waning political fortunes.[45] His message was basically a moderate one which struck a receptive chord in the people, as evidenced by the large enthusiastic crowds that turned out to hear him as he travelled throughout the country.

Some 30,000 heard de Valera wind up the Fianna Fáil campaign in Dublin on election eve. He explained that a 'comparatively moderate' programme had been adopted 'because a large section of our people have to be convinced we can do the things we set out to do. We want them to be convinced. We are giving them our pledge that we will keep exactly to the mandate we have asked for, until we come before them again. And, when we do, we know we will come before a people who will have renewed courage and who will not be frightened by any stories of bogeymen.' He emphasised that Fianna Fáil was looking to the future and forgetting about the bitterness of recent years. 'So far as we are concerned,' he declared, 'we are going to draw down a veil upon the past. That is because in looking at the past, we would only be looking at sorrowful disagreements that existed among us.'[46]

The Fianna Fáil appeal was obviously successful, because the party gained enough seats to become the largest party in the Dáil so that with the help of the Labour Party it would be able to form a government. Although there was no real doubt that the party would have sufficient parliamentary support to form a government, it was by no means certain it would be allowed to do so. There were fears, for instance, that security forces might stage a *coup d'etat* rather than allow their enemies from the civil war to assume the democratic control of the state, and those fears were by no means unjustified. In fact, the Commissioner of the Gárda Siochána, Eoin O'Duffy, who had been one of Michael Collins' most trusted lieutenants, had actually made some preliminary arrangement to stage a *coup*, but he was unable to muster sufficient backing either from the army or his own organisation to go through with his plans.[47]

When the new Dáil convened on 9 March 1932 there was a great deal of apprehension. Cosgrave obviously thought the outcome was a foregone conclusion, because he neither allowed his own name to be placed in nomination nor spoke against de Valera's nomination. The vote was taken and it was announced that the Fianna Fáil leader had been elected by 81 votes to 68. Some people in the public gallery booed, but they were drowned out by cheering as near pandamonium broke out among Fianna Fáil supporters. The President-elect then thanked the Dáil and left the chamber to receive his commission formally from the Governor-General, James MacNeill, who had taken the unprecedented step of coming to Leinster House to save de Valera the indignity of going to what had been the Vice-Regal Lodge to have his appointment confirmed by the representative of the British King.

On returning to the Dáil de Valera rose to announce his Executive Council. The paper in his hand shook as he read from it with a trembling voice.[48] It was an emotional scene; de Valera had returned from the political wilderness. He was back in power. His darkest hour was behind him.

# Notes

These notes are intended for students and those interested in doing further research. Reference is not made to sources apparent in the text. Except where otherwise noted the sources for statements and speeches are the press reports which appeared next day in the daily press. Since many of the secondary works are well-known to those involved in the field, a short title is used in the notes only in the case of lesser known and recently published works, or where the author has more than one entry cited in the bibliography, which should be used as a cross-reference to titles not listed in the notes.

## CHAPTER ONE

1. Longford and O'Neill, 90.
2. Facsimile in *Gaelic American*, 28.7.17.
3. de V., speech 26.10.17, quoted in de Valera, *Speeches and Statements by Eamon de Valera, 1917-1973*, ed. by Maurice Moynihan [hereinafter cited, Moynihan], 8.
4. Speech, Cootehill, 2.9.17, *Gaelic American*, 13.10.17.
5. *Ibid.*
6. de V. to editor, *Irish Independent*, 30.1.18.
7. Ibid.
8. Speech, Castlebar, 20.1.18, *Gaelic American*, 9.2.18.
9. de V. to editor, *Freeman's Journal*, 5.12.17.
10. de V., speech, Castlebar, 20.1.18.
11. de V. to McCartan, April 1918, *Gaelic American*, 18.5.18.
12. O'Brien, *The Irish Revolution*, 361-62; Healy, *Letters and Leaders*, 2:595-96; *Freeman's Journal*, 19.4.18.
13. *Christian Science Monitor*, 15.5.18.
14. *Ibid.*; speech, Chicago, 13.7.19, *Chicago Daily Tribune*, 14.7.19.
15. de V., 'Ireland's Case Against Conscription', ed. by Robert Brennan.
16. For extracts of Wilson's remarks regarding self-determination, see de V., *Ireland's Request to the Government of the United States of America for Recognition as a Sovereign Independent State*, 27.10.20.
17. Longford and O'Neill, 80.
18. *New York Times*, 4.3.19.
19. de V., speech, 11.4.19, Moynihan, 28.
20. Longford and O'Neill, 93.
21. *Gaelic American*, 14.6.19.
22. F. M. Carroll, *American Opinion and the Irish Question, 1910-23*, 52.
23. de V. to Griffith, 6.3.20, except where otherwise noted de Valera's correspondence in this and the next chapter is in DE2/245, State Paper Office (SPO), Dublin.
24. McCartan, *With de Valera in America*, 140.
25. Dáil, *Private Sessions*, 13.
26. Press conference, 23.6.19, *Irish Press* (Philadelphia), 28.6.19.
27. Speech, 26.9.19, *Gaelic American*, 12.7.19.
28. *Chicago Daily Tribune*, 14.7.19.
29. *Ibid.*, 15.7.19.
30. Press conference, 25.6.19, *New York Evening Post*, 25.6.19.
31. Speech, 18.7.19, *San Francisco Chronicle*, 19.7.19.
32. Speech, 29.6.19, *Gaelic American*, 12.7.19.
33. de V. to Griffith, 9.7.19.
34. *Chicago Daily Tribune*, 11.7.19.
35. *Ibid.*, 14.7.19.

36. *San Francisco Chronicle,* 19.7.19.
37. *Philadelphia Public Ledger,* 2.10.19.
38. Tansill, *America and the Fight for Irish Freedom,* 333.
39. *Irish Press* (Philadelphia), 13.9.19.
40. *New York Times,* 6.9.19.
41. Statement, New York, 17.9.19, *New York Times,* 18.9.19.
42. Statement, New York, 5.9.19, *Gaelic American,* 13.9.19.
43. *Philadelphia Public Ledger,* 2.10.19.
44. Speech, 17.10.19, *Milwaukee Journal,* 19.10.19.
45. Speech, 24.10.19, *Gaelic American,* 11.11.19.
46. Speech, 3.11.19, *Ibid.,* 15.11.19.
47. O'Doherty, *Assignment America,* 146.
48. de V. to Griffith, 19.3.20, *Irish Press* (Philadelphia), 27.3.20.
49. de V. to Griffith, 25.3.20.
50. Warren G. Harding to Frank P. Walshe, 24.3.20., O'Mara Papers, MS 21,548, National Library of Ireland (NLI).

*CHAPTER TWO*
1. *New York Times,* 24.1.20.
2. Text of interview in DE2/245, SPO.
3. *New York Globe,* 6.2.20.
4. MS of statement, n.d., in DE2/245, SPO.
5. *Gaelic American,* 13.3.20.
6. Devoy to McCartan, 21.4.19, *Gaelic American,* 30.7.21.
7. de V. to Griffith, 10.3.20.
8. de V. to Griffith, 17.2.20.
9. *Ibid.*
10. de V. to Griffith, 6.3.20.
11. de V. to Griffith, 10.3.20.
12. de V. to Griffith, 25.3.20.
13. de V. to Griffith, 9.7.19.
14. de V. to Griffith, 21.8.19.
15. Cohalan to de V., 22.2.20.
16. *Ibid.*
17. Cronin, *McGarrity Papers,* 77.
18. Tansill, 366-68; McCartney, 'De Valera in the United States', 314-15.
19. de V. to Griffith, 25.3.20.
20. *Ibid.*
21. *Ibid.*
22. *Ibid.*
23. de V. undated report presented to Dáil cabinet, June 1920, DE2/245.
24. Diarmuid O'Hegarty to de V., 8.6.20.
25. Gallagher, speech, New York, 30.7.20, *Gaelic American,* 7.8.20.
26. de V. to Gallagher, 6.8.20, *Gaelic American,* 21.8.20.
27. *Chicago Daily Tribune,* 10.6.20.
28. *Ibid.,* 11.6.20.
29. Statement, 19.6.20, *Irish Press* (Philadelphia), 26.6.20.
30. *Chicago Daily Tribune,* 12.6.20.
31. Lyons, *Ireland Since the Famine,* 399.
32. McCartan, 137.
33. Speeches, Syracuse, N.Y., 28.8.19, *Gaelic American,* 13.9.19.
34. *Freeman's Journal,* 23.5.21.
35. de V. to Griffith, 6.3.20.

36. Dáil, *Private Sessions*, 13.
37. Cronin, *McGarrity Papers*, 83.
38. de V. to Gallagher, 6.8.20, *Gaelic American*, 21.8.20.
39. *New York Times*, 11.8.20.
40. Longford and O'Neill, 114.
41. Tansill, 391.
42. *Gaelic American*, 25.9.20.
43. *Ibid.*, 9.10.20.
44. Speech, Des Moines, 7.10.20, *New York Times*, 8.1.22.
45. O'Hegarty to de V., 8.6.20.

*CHAPTER THREE*
1. Longford and O'Neill, 121.
2. Jones, *Whitehall Diary*, 3:49.
3. de V. to Brennan, 28.2.21, DE2/526, SPO.
4. Documents relating to McCartan's mission in McCartan Papers, MS. 17.682, NLI.
5. Buckley, 'The New York Irish', 372.
6. *Ibid.*, 372-74.
7. de V. to Brennan, 6.2.21, DE2/526.
8. de V., reply to questionnaire, *Gaelic American*, 26.2.21.
9. Speech, Cootehill, 2.9.17, *Gaelic American*, 31.10.17.
10. Speech, Bessborough, 28.1.18, Bromage, *De Valera and the March of a Nation*, 73; Moynihan, 62.
11. de V., reply to questionnaire, first published in *Manchester Guardian*, quoted in *Gaelic American*, 26.2.21.
12. de V., memorandum, n.d., Collins Papers.
13. I.O. [Street], *Ireland in 1921*, 59; Street, who was a British intelligence officer, quoted extensively from documents captured by the British.
14. Easter message to Irish People, April, 1921.
15. de V., response to questionnaire, *N.Y. Herald*, 17.5.21.
16. de V. to O'Brien, 14.6.21, Street, 118.
17. de V. to Boland, quoted in Boland to O'Mara, 29.2.21, O'Mara Papers, MS. 21.549, NLI.
18. *Ibid.*
19. de V. to Brennan, 28.4.21, DE2/526, SPO.
20. O'Kelly to de V., 17.4.21. *Ibid.*
21. de V. to Cáit O'Kelly, 28.4.21, *Ibid.*
22. Dáil, *Official Report for period 16-26 August 1921 and 28 February–8 June 1922*, 135.
23. O'Mara to Boland, 29.4.21, O'Mara Papers, MS. 21,549, NLI.
24. Lavelle, *James O'Mara*, 249.
25. Longford and O'Neill, 148.
26. For in-depth treatment of the differences between de Valera and Collins, see Dwyer, *Michael Collins and the Treaty*, 30-34.
27. Riddle, *Intimate Diary of the Peace Conference and After*, 228.
28. Jones, 3:69.
29. Memo. of conversation between Smuts and George V, 7.7.21, Smuts, *Selections from Smuts Papers*, 5:95-98.
30. Smuts, memo., 'De Valera's Position—Dublin Meeting', 5.7.21., *Ibid.*, 94-95.
31. Jones, 3:83.
32. Memo. of conversation between Smuts and George V, 7.7.21, *Selections from Smut's Papers*, 5:95-98.
33. *Ibid.*

34. Smuts to de V., 6.7.21; the correspondence between Smuts and de Valera in this chapter is in DE2/262. SPO.
35. de V. to Lloyd George, 13.7.21, Childers Papers, Ms. 7.790, TCD.
36. Dangerfield, *Damnable Question*, 329.
37. de V. to Collins, 15.7.21. DE2/262.
38. de V. to McGarrity, 27.12.21, *McGarrity Papers*, Ms. 17.440, NLI.
39. Lloyd George to George V, 21.7.21., Nicolson, 357.
40. Smuts to de V., 22.7.21.
41. de V. to Smuts, 31.7.21.
42. Smuts to d. V., 4.8.21.
43. de V. to McCartan, 7.2.18, Devoy Papers, MS. 18.003, NLI.
44. Dáil, *Private Session*, 29.
45. Dáil, *Debate on the Treaty*, 25; *Private Sessions*, 57.
46. de V. to Brennan, 21.5.21 and 28.2.21, DE2/526, SPO.
47. de V. to Brennan, 5.4.21, *Ibid.*
48. Dáil, *Private Sessions*, 95; de V. to McGarrity, 27.12.21.; Stack, 'Own Account of Negotiations', MS., Stack Papers; this document is extensively reproduced in Gaughan, *Austin Stack*.
49. de V. to Lord Longford, 25.2.63, enclosure in de V. to M. A. Childers, 7.12.63, R. E. Childers Papers, MS. 7.848, TCD.
50. de V. to McGarrity, 27.12.21; Stack, 'Own Account of Negotiations'; Pakenham, *Peace by Ordeal*, 83-84.
51. de V. to Longford, 25.2.63.
52. Stack, 'Own Account of Negotiations'.
53. de V. to Longford, 25.2.63.
54. K. O'Higgins, speech, Dublin, 23.8.23, *Freeman's Journal*, 24.8.23.
55. For a fuller treatment of Collins' attitude, see Dwyer, *Michael Collins and the Treaty*, 45-52.
56. de V. to McGarrity, 27.12.21.
57. Dáil, *Private Sessions*, 80, 82, 96.
58. de V. to McGarrity, 27.12.21.
59. *Ibid.*
60. Macardle, *The Irish Republic*, f.n., 530.
61. Documents relating to London Conference in DE2/304, SPO.
62. de V. to Griffith, 14.10.21; their correspondence during the conference is also in DE2/304, SPO; the drafts of Griffith's letter in his own sloping handwriting are in R. E. Childers Papers, MS. 7.790, TCD.
63. See Dwyer, *Michael Collins and the Treaty*, 65-67.
64. de V. to Griffith, 25.10.21.
65. Griffith to de V., 28.10.21.
66. Ó Murchadha, notes of cabinet meeting, 3.12.21, DE2/328, SPO.
67. Childers, 'Diary', 3.12.21, Childers Papers, MS. 7.814, TCD.
68. Stack, 'Own Account of Negotiations'.
69. Dáil, *Private Sessions*, 191; Barton to author, 1.10.69; Childers, 'Diary', 3.12.21.
70. Childers, 'Diary', 6.12.21.

*CHAPTER FOUR*
1. Mulcahy, 'Notes on Beaslaí's *Michael Collins*, Mulcahy Papers, P7/DI/67, UCD.
2. de V. to MacGarrity, 27, 12.21.
3. *Freeman's Journal*, 7.12.21.
4. de V. to McGarrity, 27.12.21.
5. Childers, Notes from cabinet meeting, 8.12.21, Childers Papers, MS. 7.819, TCD.

6. Dáil, *Debate on Treaty*, 8.
7. Childers, 'Diary', 8.12.21.
8. Dáil, *Private Sessions*, 101.
9. de V. to McGarrity, 27.12.21.
10. Childers, 'Diary', 8.12.21.
11. *Ibid*.
12. *Ibid.*, 9.12.21.
13. Dáil, *Private Sessions*, 137.
14. *Ibid.*, 153.
15. *Ibid*.
16. *Ibid.*, 186.
17. Interview with Hayden Talbot of Hearst newspapers, *Freeman's Journal*, 24.12.21; for fuller account see Talbot, *Michael Collins' Own Story*, 231-34.
18. *Ibid*.
19. Dáil, *Private Sessions*, 216, 139.
20. Dáil, *Debate on Treaty*, 25.
21. Dáil, *Private Sessions*, 123.
22. Dáil, *Debate on Treaty*, 32.
23. de V. to McGarrity, 10.9.22.
24. For more on these overtures, see Dwyer, *Michael Collins and the Treaty*, 130-34.
25. Gaughan, *Thomas Johnson*, 194-95.
26. Hayes, 'Dáil Éireann and the Irish Civil War', *Studies*, 58, 5-6.
27. Dáil, *Debate on Treaty*, 259.
28. *Ibid.*, 274.
29. Dáil, *Private Sessions*, 110.
30. *Ibid.*, 102.
31. de V. to McGarrity, 27.12.21.
32. Dáil, *Debate on Treaty*, 281.
33. *Ibid.*, 303.
34. *New York Times*, 7.1.22.
35. *Ibid.*, 7.12.21.
36. *Ibid.*, 9.12.21.
37. Dáil, *Debate on Treaty*, 346.
38. *Freeman's Journal*, 9.1.22.
39. Dáil, *Debate on Treaty*, 347.
40. Beaslaí, *Michael Collins*, 2:349.
41. Dáil, *Debate on Treaty*, 347.
42. Childers, Minutes of meeting, 8.1.22.
43. Dáil, *Debate on Treaty*, 349.
44. *Ibid.*, 352.
45. *Ibid.*, 353.
46. *Ibid.*, 356.
47. *Ibid.*, 375.
48. *Ibid.*, 377.
49. *Ibid.*, 379.
50. *Ibid.*, 399.
51. *Ibid.*, 410.
52. Press conference, 11.1.22, *Freeman's Journal*, 12.1.22.
53. Interview, 15.1.22, *Poblacht na h-Éireann*, 17.1.22.
54. O'Hegarty, *A History of Ireland under the Union*, 786.
55. Speech, Cork, 19.2.22, *Irish Independent*, 20.2.22.
56. Speech, Ennis, 25.2.22, *Freeman's Journal*, 27.2.22.
57. de V. to Griffith, 10.3.22.
58. *Irish Independent*, 18.3.22.

59. Moynihan, 98.
60. *Ibid.*, 99.
61. Curran, *Birth of the Irish Free State*, 174-75.
62. Beaslaí, 2:369.
63. de V., speech, Sinn Féin Árd Fheis, 21.2.22, *Poblacht na h-Éireann*, 28.2.22.
64. Macardle, 678.
65. Moynihan, 100.
66. Interview, 10.4.22, Macardle, 699-700.
67. Interviewed by *Manchester Guardian*, 11.4.22, *Poblacht na h-Éireann*, 20.4.22.
68. Interview, 11.4.22, Macardle, 700.
69. Collins, speech, Wexford, 9.4.22, *Freeman's Journal*, 10.4.22.
70. de V., statement, 12.4.22, *Freeman's Journal*, 13.4.22.
71. Seanad, *Debates*, 20:1876.
72. Speech in Dáil, 14.10.31, Moynihan, 185.
73. Proclamation, 16.4.22, *Poblacht na h-Éireann*, 20.4.22.
74. O'Brien, *Forth the Banners Go*, 219-20.
75. MacSwiney to Mulcahy, 24.4.22, Mary MacSwiney Papers, UCD.
76. *Freeman's Journal*, 27.4.22.
77. Younger, *A State of Disunion*, 146.
78. de V., statement, 1.5.22, *Irish Independent*, 2.5.22.
79. de V., statement, 2.5.22, *Poblacht na h-Éireann*, 4.5.22.
80. Interviewed by John Steele, *Poblacht na h-Éireann*, 18.5.22.
81. de V. to Hearne, 13.5.22, Hearne Papers, MS. 15.987, NLI.
82. Dáil, *Official Report*, (17.5.22), 426.
83. *Ibid.*, 440.
84. Towey, 'The Reaction of the British Government to the 1922 Collins—de Valera Pact', *Irish Historical Studies*, 22:73.
85. de V. to Griffith, 16.10.21, DE2/304.
86. Collins, speech, Cork, 14.6.22, *Irish Independent*, 15.6.22.
87. *Irish Independent*, 22.6.22.
88. Churchill, speech, 26.6.22.

## CHAPTER FIVE

1. de V., statement, 26.6.22, Moynihan, 107.
2. de V., speech, Fianna Fáil Árd Fheis, October 1931.
3. de V. to Brugha, 6.7.22, MacSwiney Papers, UCD.
4. *The Free State*, 8.7.22.
5. Brennan, *Allegiance*, 352.
6. Peter Golden, *Impressions of Ireland*, 54.
7. de V., 'Diary', 13.8.22, Longford and O'Neill, 198.
8. Erskine Childers to Molly Childers, 12.7.22.
9. Deasy, *Brother Against Brother*, 76-77.
10. Neeson, *Civil War in Ireland*, 265; Deasy, 77-78.
11. Neeson, *Life and Death of Michael Collins*, 136.
12. Williams, 'From Treaty to Civil War', in *The Irish Struggle*, 124.
13. Longford and O'Neill, 199; Mulcahy's account in Mulcahy Papers, P7D/65/22/20, UCD.
14. de V. to McGarrity, 10.9.22.
15. *Ibid.*
16. de V. to Cathal Ó Murchadha, 7.9.22.
17. *Ibid.*
18. *Ibid.*, 6.9.22.
19. *Ibid.*

20. Statement issued by O. Traynor, B. Mellows, E. Corbett, L. Pilkington, T. Barry, and P. Ó Domhnaill, 9.9.22.
21. de V. to Ó Murchadha, 11.9.22.
22. *Ibid.*, 13.9.22.
23. *Ibid.*, 12.9.22.
24. de V. to McGarrity, 10.9.22.
25. *Ibid.*
26. *Ibid.*, 12.10.22.
27. *Ibid.*
28. *Freeman's Journal*, 11.10.22.
29. Proposal prepared by de Valera for Executive meeting, 17.10.22.
30. de V. to McGarrity, 19.10.21.
31. *Freeman's Journal*, 3.11.22.
32. de V. and P. Ruttledge, Proclamations quoted in *Freeman's Journal*, 21, 23.11.22.
33. de V. to Mary MacSwiney, n.d. November 1922, Childers Papers, MS. 7.835, TCD.
34. de V. to McGarrity, 28.11.22.
35. de V. to Molly Childers, 11.11.22.
36. de V. to Mary MacSwiney, n.d. November 1922.
37. de V. to McGarrity, 28.11.22.
38. de V. to Molly Childers, n.d. November 1922, Childers Papers, Ms. 7.848, TCD.
39. *Ibid.*, 20.11.22.
40. *Freeman's Journal*, 24.11.22.
41. de V. to Sinéad de Valera, 27.11.22, Childers Papers, MS. 7.848, TCD.
42. de V. to Mary MacSwiney, 24.11.22.
43. de V. to McGarrity, 28.11.22.
44. Lynch to M. Hayes, 27.11.22, *Freeman's Journal*, 9.12.22.
45. de V. to Lynch, 11.12.22, Longford and O'Neill, 208.
46. de V. to Ruttledge, 15.12.22, *Ibid.*
47. de V. to Lynch, 18.12.22, *Ibid.*, 209.
48. Deasy, *Brother Against Brother*, 115.
49. Gaughan, *Austin Stack*, 230.
50. de V. to McGarrity, 5.2.23.
51. de V. to Lynch, 2.2.23, Longford and O'Neill, 213.
52. de V. to J. J. O'Kelly, 5.2.23.
53. *New York Times* quoting the *Morning Post*, both 24.1.23.
54. de V. to McGarrity, 5.2.23.
55. de V. to Lynch, 7.2.23, Longford and O'Neill, 213.
56. Curtis to Jones, 28.6.28, Jones, 3:222.
57. *Irish Independent*, 9.2.23.
58. O'Higgins, interview, 3.2.23, *Freeman's Journal*, 5.2.23.
59. Letter from Mary MacSwiney seized and published, *Freeman's Journal*, 19.2.23.
60. INS report, *Freeman's Journal*, 17.2.23.
61. Press Association report, *Freeman's Journal*, 17.2.23.
62. de V. to Edith Ellis, 26.2.23.
63. Lynch to de V., 28.2.23, Longford and O'Neill, 215.
64. de V. to Lynch, 7.3.23, *Ibid.*, 216.
65. de V. to Mary MacSwiney, 14.3.23.
66. Longford and O'Neill, 217-18.
67. *Irish Independent*, 12.3.23.
68. Longford and O'Neill, 219.
69. de V. to Ruttledge, 11.4.23, *Ibid.*

# DE VALERA'S DARKEST HOUR

70. de V., Address to Army, 12.4.23, *Éire*, 28.4.23.
71. de V., Proclamation, 27.4.23.
72. Seanad, *Debates*, 1:1018-26.
73. Dáil, *Debates*, 40:360.
74. *Éire*, 19.5.23.
75. Dáil, *Debates*, 40:290.
76. de V. to Molly Childers, 21.6.23.
77. *Éire*, 7.7.23.
78. de V. to press, 20.7.23, *Éire*, 28.7.23.
79. Interviewed by W. H. Brayden, 20.7.23, *Irish Independent*, 23.7.23.
80. de V. to press, 19.7.23, *Éire*, 28.7.23.
81. *Freeman's Journal*, 22.7.23.
82. *Irish Independent*, 24.7.23.
83. de V. to Molly Childers, 31.7.23.
84. *Éire*, 1.9.23.
85. *Irish Independent*, 16.8.23.
86. *Philadelphia Public Ledger*, 18.8.23.
87. *Freeman's Journal*, 17.8.23.
88. C.B. O'C. to David Nelligan, 23.8.23; Nelligan to Mulcahy, 23.8.23, S1-369/15, SPO.
89. *Baltimore Sun*, 16.8.23.
90. V. de Valera, speech, 19.8.23, *Éire*, 25.8.23.
91. Blanche to R. Poincaré, 30.8.23, Tierney, 'Calandar of Irelande', *Collectanea Hibernica*, No. 23, 120.

## CHAPTER SIX

1. O'Neill, 'In Search of a Political Path: Irish Republicanism, 1922 to 1927', *Historical Studies*, 10:157.
2. Comhairle na dTeachtai, minutes, 7.8.24, quoted in Gaughan, *Austin Stack*, 321-22.
3. *Ibid.*, 323.
4. *Ibid.*, 329.
5. *Ibid.*, 335.
6. Moynihan, 115-16.
7. Speech in Dundalk, 24.8.24.
8. de V. to Mary MacSwiney, 7.8.23.
9. de V., Statement, 13.10.24.
10. *Irish News and Belfast Morning News*, 3.11.24.
11. de V., statement, 6.12.25, Moynihan, 122-25.
12. *An Phoblacht*, 20.11.25.
13. McInerny, 'Gerry Boland's Story as told to Michael McInerny', *Irish Times*, 10.10.68.
14. Moynihan, 127.
15. de V. to A. Ford, 27.5.26, O'Neill, *Historical Studies*, 10:161.
16. *An Phoblacht*, 16.4.26.
17. Mary MacSwiney to Seán T. O'Kelly, 8.6.26.
18. *Ibid.*
19. *Ibid.*
20. *An Phoblacht*, 9.4.26.
21. de V., interview, 17.4.26, Moynihan, 131.
22. *Ibid.*, 133-39.
23. MacSwiney to editor, *Irish Independent*, 15.6.26.
24. *New York Times*, 6.3.27.
25. *Ibid.*, 15.3.27.

26. Speech, 3.4.27, *Irish World* (New York), 16.4.27.
27. Speech, Boston, *Ibid.*, 7.5.27.
28. *Irish Times,* 11.7.27.
29. Statement, 11.7.27, Moynihan, 149.
30. Speech, Dublin, 26.7.27, *Irish Times,* 27.7.27.
31. de V. to J. J. Hearne, 29.4.28, Hearne Papers, MS. 15.987, NLI.
32. Dáil, *Debates,* 41:1101.
33. Johnson, memo., 2.8.27, Gaughan, *Thomas Johnson,* 303.
34. Statement, 10.8.27, Moynihan, 150.
35. Dáil, *Debates,* 41:1102.
36. *Ibid.*
37. *Ibid.,* 23:2486-87, *New York Times,* 1.6.28.
38. de V., speech, 2.5.29, Moynihan, 171.
39. Interview, 10.12.29, *Irish World,* 21.12.29.
40. Interview, *Irish World,* 28.12.29; Speech, Staten Island, 26.1.30, *Ibid.,* 1.2.30.
41. Blanche to Poincaré, 15.10.24, Tiernay, 126.
42. Keatinge, *The Formulation of Irish Foreign Policy,* 17.
43. Cosgrave, speech, Tralee, 31.1.32, *The Kerryman,* 6.2.32.
44. Fianna Fáil Manifesto, 9.2.32, Moynihan, 190.
45. de V., speech, 10.2.32, *The Kerryman,* 13.2.32.
46. de V., speech, 15.2.32, *Irish Press,* 16.2.32.
47. Brady, *Guardians of the Peace,* 167-69.
48. *Irish Press,* 10.3.32.

# Bibliography

*MANUSCRIPT SOURCES:*

Robert Barton, Assorted Papers, Trinity College, Dublin.
R. Erskine Childers Papers, Trinity College, Dublin.
Michael Collins, Assorted Papers in possession of Liam Collins, Clonakilty, County Cork.
Dáil Éireann Files, State Paper Office, Dublin Castle, Dublin.
John Devoy Papers, National Library of Ireland, Dublin.
John J. Hearne Papers, National Library of Ireland, Dublin.
Patrick McCartan Papers, National Library of Ireland, Dublin.
Joseph McGarrity Papers, National Library of Ireland, Dublin.
Mary MacSwiney Papers, University College, Dublin.
Richard Mulcahy Papers, University College, Dublin.
Kathleen Napoli (née McKenna) Papers, National Library of Ireland, Dublin.
James O'Mara Papers, National Library of Ireland, Dublin.
Austin Stack Papers, in possession of Nanette Barrett, Tralee, County Kerry.

*NEWSPAPERS AND PERIODICALS:*

*An Phoblacht, Baltimore Sun, Chicago Daily Tribune, Christian Science Monitor, Daily Mail, Éire, Freeman's Journal, Gaelic American, Irish Free State, Irish Independent, Irish News and Belfast Morning News, Irish Press* (Dublin), *Irish Press* (Philadelphia), *Irish Times, Irish World* (New York), *The Kerryman, Manchester Guardian, Milwaukee Journal, Morning Post, New York Evening Post, New York Globe, New York Herald, New York Times, The Observer, Philadelphia Public Ledger, Poblacht na h-Éireann, San Francisco Chronicle, Sunday Press, The Times* (London).

*BOOKS AND ARTICLES:*

Bailey, Thomas A., *Woodrow Wilson and the Great Betrayal*, New York, 1945.
Beaslaí, Piaras, *Michael Collins and the Making of a New Ireland*, 2 vols., Dublin, 1926.
Boyce, D. G., *Englishmen and Irish Troubles: British Opinion and the Making of Irish Policy, 1918-1922*, London, 1972.
Boyle, Andrew, *The Riddle of Erskine Childers*, London, 1977.
Brady, Conor, *Guardians of the Peace*, Dublin, 1974.
Brennan, Robert, *Allegiance*, Dublin, 1950.
Bromage, Mary C., *De Valera and the March of a Nation*, London, 1956.
Buckley, John Patrick, 'The New York Irish: Their View of American Foreign Policy, 1914-1921', Ph.D. thesis, New York University, 1974.

Carroll, F. M. *American Opinion and the Irish Question, 1910-1923,* Dublin, 1978.
Colum, Padraic, *Arthur Griffith,* Dublin, 1959.
Cronin, Seán, *Irish Nationalism: A History of Its Roots and Ideology,* Dublin 1980.
——, *The McGarrity Papers,* Tralee, 1972.
Dáil Éireann, *Official Report: Debate on the Treaty between Great Britain and Ireland,* Dublin, 1922.
——, Official Report: For Periods 16th August, 1921 to 26th August, 1921, and 28th February, 1922 to 8th June, 1922.
——, *Private Sessions of Second Dáil,* Dublin, n.d.
Dangerfield, George, *Damnable Question,* London, 1977.
Deasy, Liam, *Brother Against Brother,* Dublin & Cork, 1982.
de Valera, Eamon, *Ireland's Case Against Conscription,* Dublin, 1918.
——, *Ireland's Request to the Government of the United States of America for Recognition as a Sovereign Independent State,* New York, 1920.
——, *Speeches and Statements by Eamon de Valera, 1917-1973,* ed. by Maurice Moynihan, Dublin, 1980.
Dwyer, T. Ryle, *De Valera's Finest Hour, 1932-1959,* Dublin & Cork, 1982.
——, *Michael Collins and the Treaty,* Dublin & Cork, 1981.
Figgis, Darrell, *Recollection of the Irish War,* London, 1927.
Fitz-Gerald, William, *The Voice of Ireland,* Dublin, 1924.
Gallagher, Frank, *The Anglo-Irish Treaty,* London, 1965.
Gaughan, J. Anthony, *Austin Stack,* Dublin, 1977.
——, *Thomas Johnson,* Dublin, 1980.
Harkness, D. W., 'Britain and the Independence of the Dominions', in Moody, T. W., ed., *Nationality and the Pursuit of Independence,* 141-159.
——, *The Restless Dominion,* Dublin, 1969.
Hayes, Michael, 'Dáil Éireann and the Irish Civil War', *Studies,* 58 (Spring 1969), 1-24.
Healy, T. M., *Letters and Leaders of My Day,* London, n.d.
Jones, Thomas, *Whitehall Diary,* Vol. 3, *Ireland, 1918-1925,* London, 1971.
Keatinge, Richard, *The Formulation of Irish Foreign Policy,* Dublin, 1973.
Lavelle, Patricia, *James O'Mara,* Dublin, 1961.
Longford, Earl of, 'The Treaty Negotiations', in Williams, Desmond, *The Irish Struggle,* 107-115.
——, and O'Neill, Thomas, *Eamon de Valera,* Dublin, 1970.
Lyons, F. S. L., *Ireland Since the Famine,* London, 1971.
Macardle, Dorothy, *The Irish Republic,* Dublin, 1937.
McCartan, Patrick, *With de Valera in America,* Dublin, 1932.
McColgan, 'Implementing the 1921 Treaty: Lionel Curtis and Constitutional Procedure', *Irish Historical Studies,* 20:312-333.
Midleton, Earl of, *Records and Reactions, 1856-1939,* London, 1939.

Moody, T. W., ed., *Nationality and the Pursuit of National Independence*, Dublin, 1980.
Moynihan, Maurice, see de Valera, Eamon.
Murdoch, R., Interview with Robert Barton, *Sunday Press*, September-October, 1971.
Neeson, Eoin, *The Civil War in Ireland, 1922-1923*, Cork, 1966.
——, *The Life and Death of Michael Collins*, Cork, 1968.
Nicolson, Harold, *King George V*, London, 1952.
O'Brien, William, *Forth the Banners Go*, Dublin, 1969.
O'Brien, William, *The Irish Revolution and How It Came About*, London, 1923.
O'Connor, Frank, *The Big Fellow*, Dublin, 1965.
O'Connor, Ulick, *Oliver St. John Gogarty*, London, 1964.
O'Doherty, Katherine, *Assignment America*, New York, 1957.
Ó Faoláin, Seán, *De Valera*, London, 1939.
O'Hegarty, P. S., *A History of Ireland Under the Union, 1801-1922*, London, 1952.
O'Malley, Ernie, *On Another Man's Wound*, Dublin, 1936.
——, *The Singing Flame*, Dublin, 1978.
O'Neill, Thomas, 'In Search of a Political Path: Irish Republicanism 1922-1927', *Historical Studies*, 10 (1976), 147-171.
O'Sullivan, Donal, *The Irish Free State and Its Senate*, London, 1940.
Pakenham, Frank (later Longford, Earl of), *Peace by Ordeal*, London, 1935.
Phillips, W. Alison, *The Revolution in Ireland, 1906-1923*, London, 1926.
Riddell, Lord, *Intimate Diary of the Peace Conference and After*, London, 1933.
Smuts, J. C., *Selections from Smut's Papers*, Vol. 5, London, 1973.
Street, C. J. C., *Ireland in 1921*, London, 1921.
Tansill, Charles, C., *America and the Fight for Irish Freedom, 1866-1922*, New York, 1957.
Tierney, Mark, 'Calandar of Irlande', *Collectanea Hibernica*, No. 23, 116-146.
Towey, Thomas, 'The Reaction of the British Government to the 1922 Collins-de Valera Pact', *Irish Historical Studies*, 22:65-76.
Taylor, Rex, *Michael Collins*, London, 1958.
Ward, Alan J., *Ireland and Anglo-American Relations, 1899-1921*, London, 1969.
Williams, T. Desmond, 'From Free State to Civil War', in Williams, T. Desmond, ed., *The Irish Struggle*, London, 1966.
Younger, Carlton, *Ireland's Civil War*, London, 1968.
——, *A State of Disunion*, London, 1972.

# Index

Ackerman, Carl, 61
Aiken, Frank, 141, 154
Ancient Order of Hibernians, 19
Anglo-Irish Treaty (1921), 7, 62, 80-105, 107, 110-14, 116-17, 122-23, 126, 128, 137, 142-43, 151-53, 158, 160, 167, 169
American Association for Recognition of Irish Republic (AARIR), 51, 95
Austria, 43

Ballyseedy Cross, 138
Bandon, 163
Barrett, Dick, 132
Barton, Robert, 69, 71-74, 79, 81-83
Béalnabláth, 121, 123
Belgium, 31
Benedict XV, Pope, 54, 76
Berne, 56
Blanche, Alfred, 148
Boland, Gerry, 155
Boland, Harry, 15, 42, 58, 94-95, 120
Bonar Law, Andrew, 53, 55
Borah, Sen. William, 17, 36, 45
Boston, 19, 21, 43, 162
Boundary Commission, 79, 143-44, 151-53, 156, 167-68
Brennan, Robert, 43, 53, 55, 120
Brugha, Cathal, 19-20, 22, 60, 69, 71, 80, 83, 95, 109-10, 115, 120

Cahirciveen, 138
Canada, 65, 78, 80, 88, 170
Cavan, 107
Chicago, 19-20, 22, 43-46, 48-49
*Chicago Daily Tribune,* 22, 45-46, 106, 111
Childers, Erskine, 43, 73, 75, 80, 82, 84, 121, 130-31, 148
Childers, Molly, 130
China, 25
*Christian Science Monitor,* 12
Churchill, Winston S., 61, 110, 113, 116-17, 170
Clan-na-Gael, 33, 93
Cobh, 161
Cohalan, Daniel, 23, 33-40, 44-48, 51, 92-95
Collins, Michael, 15, 60-61, 69, 71-72, 76, 79-80, 82-83, 88-91, 94-102, 106-7, 109-11, 113-15, 117-22, 130, 153, 160, 167, 172
*Comhairle na dTeachtaí,* 150, 155, 157-58
Connolly, Tom, 30
Cork, 114
Cosgrave, W. T., 69, 71, 83, 119, 135, 140-41, 143, 162, 164-65, 170-72
Craig, Sir James, 62-63, 67-68
Cromwell, Oliver, 64
Cuba, 30-31, 33, 70
Cumann na mBan, 147
Cumann na nGaedheal, 147-48, 162, 164-66

## DE VALERA'S DARKEST HOUR

Cumann na Poblachta, 97, 103, 105
Curran, Prof. Joseph M., 104
Curtis, Lionel, 135

*Daily Chronicle*, 168
*Daily Express*, 168
*Daily Herald*, 9
*Daily Mail*, 134, 168
de Valera, Eamon, *passim*
    and Árd Fheis agreement (1922), 102-3, 114
    Article X, 21, 24-27, 166
    Article XI, 24-25, 27
    conscription, 12-14
    Draft Treaty A, 74-75
    Document No. 2, 84-86, 88-94, 113-14, 126-27, 137, 142, 146, 154
    Dominion Status, 55, 63, 65-67, 72, 80
    election pact with Collins, 113-14, 116, 119, 122-23
    Emergency Government, 128, 141-42, 149-50, 154, 157-59
    External Association, 65, 70, 74-75, 77-78, 80-81, 87, 92, 95, 102, 155
    German Plot, 13, 16
    Irish-Americans, 10, 17-19, 22-24, 28, 33, 35, 37, 39-42, 48, 51-52, 161, 169
    land annuities, 156, 167, 171
    neutrality, 13, 31, 58, 75, 114
    oath, 79-80, 86-87, 93, 140-41, 155-56, 158-59, 162-65, 168, 171
    partition (Ulster) question, 55-57, 62, 64, 66-69, 86, 90, 123, 130, 142-44, 151-54, 159, 166, 168
    propaganda, 17, 20, 43, 50, 53-54, 58, 94, 112, 131, 161
    Republican bonds, 18, 35-36, 40, 60
    self-determination, 10-11, 14-16, 25, 27, 47, 58, 67, 112
    talk of civil war, 97, 99, 103-4, 117
    visits to United States, 15-52, 160-62, 168-69
de Valera, Sinéad, 131
de Valera, Vivion, 148
Deasy, Liam, 121-22, 133-34
Delaware, 18
Democratic Party (USA), 36, 40-41, 46
Denmark, 43
Denver, 27
Devoy, John, 23, 33-34, 37-38, 40-41, 44, 46, 48, 50-51
Document No. 2, see under de Valera, Eamon
Douglas, James, 140
Duffy, George Gavan, 72, 75, 79, 82
Duggan, Eamon, 72, 79
Dun Laoghaire, 105-6
Dundalk, 152,
Dungarvan, 103

Easter Rebellion, 9, 33, 61, 108
Egypt, 38
*Éire*, 141
Ennis, 102, 145, 151, 160, 162
External Association, see under de Valera, Eamon

Fianna Fáil, 159-68, 171-73
FitzGerald, Desmond, 144, 170

France, 10, 16, 23, 25, 43, 169
*Freeman's Journal,* 91, 96
Friends of Irish Freedom (FOIF), 17, 23-24, 33-35, 37, 44, 48-51, 95
Four Courts, 108-9, 116-18, 121

*Gaelic American,* 23, 32-33, 37-38, 41, 46
Gaelic League, 160
Gallagher, Bishop Michael J., 44-45, 48
Geneva, 56
George V, King, 76, 87
Germany, 16, 28, 43, 75, 169, 171
Government of Ireland Act (1920), see Partition Act
Griffith, Arthur, 10, 15, 28, 39, 41, 49, 69, 71-72, 76, 79-83, 88, 90-91, 98-101, 103, 106-7, 109-11, 118-20, 144
Harding, Warren G., 50-51
Hayes, Archbishop Patrick J., 54

India, 38
International News Service, 136
*Irish Bulletin,* 43
Irish Convention, 68
*Irish Independent,* 104, 144
Irish Parliamentary Party, 12, 14-15
*Irish Press* (Dublin), 169
*Irish Press* (Philadelphia), 32-33
Irish Republican Army (IRA) and Irreguiars, 53, 61, 103-6, 108-12, 115-16, 118-27, 130, 132, 134, 137, 141, 146, 154
Irish Republican Brotherhood (IRB), 33, 71-72, 93, 104
Irish Volunteers, 33, 155
*Irish World* (New York), 32
Italy, 43

Jameson, Andrew, 140
Johnson, Sen. Hiram, 41, 45
Johnson, Thomas, 163-65

Kellog-Briande Pact, 166
Kerensky, Alexander, 10, 171
Killarney, 138

Labour Party, 59, 108-9, 115, 119, 163, 165, 172
League of Nations, 16, 18, 20-24, 27-29, 31, 34, 37, 49, 75, 166, 169
Lemass, Noel, 145
Lemass, Seán, 159 f.n.
Limerick, 81
Lincoln Jail, 13-15
Lloyd George, David, 53, 58-59, 62-68, 70-71, 73, 81, 88, 92, 107, 153, 167
Logue, William Cardinal, 54
Lynch, Liam, 115-16, 121-22, 125, 132-35, 137-39

McCartan, Patrick, 33, 45, 47-48, 51, 54
McGarrity, Joseph, 33-34, 39, 48, 122, 126, 133-35, 142
McKelvey, Joe, 116, 132
MacNeill, James, 173
MacSwiney, Alice, 130

MacSwiney, Mary, 96, 110, 129-30, 136-38, 152, 156-58, 160
MacSwiney, Terence, 129
Manchester, New Hampshire, 19
Maryland, 18
Mason, William, 30, 42
Massachusetts, 18-19
Mellows, Liam, 132
Milwaukee, 26
Monroe Doctrine, 31-32, 38, 58
Montana, 18-19
*Morning Post,* 153
Mulcahy, Richard, 104, 110, 122, 147

New Jersey, 18
New Orleans, 43
New York, 18-19, 21, 26, 30, 39-40, 47, 49-50, 54, 160, 168
*New York Globe,* 32
New York Supreme Court, 161
*New York Times,* 94
Northern Ireland, 62, 65, 69, 79, 86, 99, 153, 155, 166, see also Partition Act and partition question under de Valera, Eamon

O'Connor, Art, 157-59
O'Connor, Rory, 104-5, 108, 116, 125, 132
O'Duffy, Eoin, 172
O'Flanagan, Michael, 157
O'Higgins, Kevin, 113, 133, 135, 138-39, 147, 163
O'Kelly, Cáit, 59
O'Kelly, J. J., 134-35
O'Kelly, Seán T., 59-60, 90, 158, 165
O'Mara, James, 60

Partition Act (1920), 55-57, 88, 99, 101, 167
Peace Conference (Paris), 9-10, 15-17, 27
Phelan, Sen. James D., 36
Philadelphia, 23, 26
Platt Amendment, 31-33, 75
Plunkett, George N. Count, 15, 69-70
Press Association, 137

Rathmines, 147
Republican Party (USA), 36, 40-41, 44-46, 92
Roman Catholic hierarchy, 12, 110, 127
Roosevelt, Franklin D., 36
Russia (see also Soviet Union), 10, 25
Ruttledge, Patrick, 90, 139, 149

San Francisco, 19, 21-22, 43, 46
St Louis, 27
St Paul, 161
Sabastini, Monsignor, 54
Sinn Féin, 9-15, 20, 47, 55, 58, 61, 65-66, 71, 94, 102, 109, 114-15, 119, 126, 134, 139, 142, 144-45, 148, 152, 154-57, 160, 162
Smuts, J. C., 61-63, 66-68, 81, 89
Spain, 23, 25, 43

South Africa, Union of, 43, 51, 54, 63, 65
Soviet Union (USSR), 43, 51, 54, 57, 75
Stack, Austin, 60, 69, 71, 83
Steele, John, 106
Switzerland, 43, 56, 75

Thurles, 103
Transvaal Republic, 63
Tralee, 144, 171
Turner, Bishop William, 39

Ultimate Financial Settlement (1926), 156, 167
United States of America, 9-11, 13-15, 17-53, 55, 60-61, 70, 75, 94, 111-12, 119, 134, 158, 160-62, 168-69
U.S. House of Representatives, 15, 30, 42
U.S. Senate, 17, 25, 27-29, 36, 38, 111

Vatican, 76, 128, 169
Versailles Treaty (1919), 16, 18-21, 23, 27-30, 38, 71
Virginia, 18

Walsh, Sen. Thomas, 27
Washington, D.C., 43, 51
Westminster, Statute of, 170
*Westminster Gazette,* 31-33, 37, 59
Wexford, 106
Williams, Prof. T. Desmond, 122
Wilson, Sir Henry, 116
Wilson, Pres. Woodrow, 9-12, 14-19, 22, 24-28, 34, 36-37, 44, 50-51, 71

Zurich, 56